Unwavering

Vicki H Gwin

Step in to the Adventure.

D1367952

For Allison
with love!
What a wonderful
journey we have
had together — I
can't wait to see
where your life takes
you! It WILL
be an adventure!
Mrs. Vuki
XO

VICKI HALL GWIN

Dedication

This is for all who dare to dream.   And for all who dare to be intentional about making their dreams happen. God is the Giver of Dreams. And by trusting in Him, our lives will be richer, fuller and more adventurous than we (in all of our small imaginings) could have ever dreamed.

You may not see your name here, anywhere in this manuscript, but I assure you, if you know me, you are a HUGE part of my story. Who can describe how one life affects another life? We share a moment, or a day, or a lifetime together, and we are irreversibly different because of that interaction we had.

My prayer is that, as you read this account of one life, you will notice HIM more than you notice me. This is the story of His work in my life. May you come to believe, as you read, that **He also wants to do great things in your life**, as you trust in Him.

Dream on!

CONTENTS

VICKI HALL GWIN

This is just for you.

If you're a missionary,

   . . . or an aspiring one.

If you struggle with chronic illness.

If you want to learn how to walk by faith.

If you have children.

If you're in fulltime ministry.

If you're scared and lonely.

If you live in a family.

If you are living outside of your culture.

If you just plain want to love Jesus more.

If you need meaning in your life today.

Dream a little dream with me.

Thanks.

All thanks be to the Lord Jesus Christ. He pursued my soul, and wouldn't let up, until my life was His, and His alone.   He is the reason I get out of bed every morning. He has given me purpose and meaning.   And HOPE.

Special Mention:

To Elizabeth St. Denis, my daughter, who inspired me with her incredible cover painting (at age 10) - a picture of us walking "into the adventure", which was both scary and exciting at the same time. Thank you for your creativity and for the taking my photograph for the back cover. Your talents constantly inspire me.

To Anne, who made me constant cups of hot tea and served them with lovely, encouraging words. You are the best.

To Ginger Arnold, who read the manuscript before publication, (along with many others) and encouraged and inspired me along the way. Your heart and your ability to see truth clearly have lightened my load tremendously.

To Karen Furr, who made this possible by coaching me through the unknown waters of writing a rather large manuscript and publishing.   You helped make my dreams come true.

Let's make an effort to go
where we might not normally go, in order to meet
people we might not normally meet,
in order to invite them to meet our God.

If giving this book will help you do that,
then please share it with others!

VICKI HALL GWIN

Introduction.

Location: English Bay Cafe.

There I sat, gazing moony-eyed across the table at my husband of 3 days.

"So," he said, "when are you going to write your first book?"

"I think I want to live a little first," I said shyly. "You know, gain some life experiences, have some adventures." I knew in that moment that my life was going to be amazing, and that walking with an amazing God would teach me more than I could ever dream. I knew that the people I would meet and the places I would go, would exceed even THIS dreamer's hopes. I had no idea, however, just how MUCH God would exceed my dreams.

But it was calling to me.

To step into the adventure.

VICKI HALL GWIN

Chapter, the First.

The Early Years.

"You feel the wind in your hair, you watch the
seagulls soar by . . . "   (*Carole's Song - VHG)*

I was born on June 15th, 1961.   My Mom drove
herself to the hospital, in the middle of the night,
because my dad was working night shift at the fire
hall.   My big sister was almost 10, and able to
manage the other 3 sleeping children. The doctor
came to the hospital in his pyjamas to deliver me.
Or so I've been told.   My other sister cried with
happiness because I was a girl.

Location: White Rock, British Columbia, Canada.
We lived two miles from the American border and
right on the Pacific Ocean. I was blessed to start out

in such a family, and in such a beautiful and blessed part of the world.

I have always been INTENTIONAL. This was my favourite word long before society starting using it as a trendy catch-phrase. I think it goes back to even before I could talk. My mother probably noticed it before I did.

I was a head banger. It's a little embarrassing to admit. One of my mother's church friends sewed me a padded helmet, so that I would not hurt myself, banging my head against the side of the crib. Since I'm a musician, I prefer to think that I always had a song in my head, and was just keeping time to the music. Nevertheless, for whatever reason, I was born with internal motivation and always felt it. I was going somewhere and I wanted everyone to know it.

I remember being 4 or 5 years old, watching ants on the sidewalk, outside of our White Rock home. They were carrying crumbs larger than themselves, single file, to their ant hill home. They were being intentional, and I remember being fascinated by them.

As the youngest of 5, I grew up surrounded by excellent music. My dad, was an amazing musician, trained in the Salvation Army by his dad who was the bandmaster (who in turn had been taught by his dad who played in the band and so on and so forth for generations). Dad taught his family well and by the time I came along, the "Hall Family Band" was in existence, performing 52 weeks of the year, at evening services all over the Lower Mainland. When I was old enough I joined them, as the triangle player.   There was never a day in my life when music did not feature greatly in it.   Dad let me play his euphonium, his drum kit, and over the years provided me with a clarinet, autoharp, harmonicas and a piano to learn.   He would sit me down in front of the old stereo, put the big headphones on my head, and instruct me what instrument to listen for.   I loved every minute of it and learned to love the brass band music as much as he did.

When I was little, I was expected to be cute & entertaining. When my brothers and sisters had parties, I learned to sing on command, to dance with the 45 vinyl's, and to never tell their secrets! When I was old enough to start kindergarten, my mother went back to work at the post office, and I went a lot of places with my older brothers and sisters. Yes, at five years old I remember hitch-hiking, and making all sorts of "interesting" memories. This plethora of stories and experiences were the secrets that my brothers and sisters made me promise never to tell!

Having grown up in a house near the beautiful ocean, I still say that the Ocean is my "Happy Place." A girl can't grow up with a view of the ocean and the freedom to walk there daily, without that being her favourite place!   There was only the massive Oxford Hill in between my beloved ocean and I. Oxford Hill is not just any hill. With a 23% gradient, walking up it is like climbing a mountain. Almost every day we would walk down the hill to the ocean and then of course have to walk back up the steep incline to get home. I remember many times standing at the bottom of the hill and imagining myself already at the top!   This was one of my first lessons on how to be intentional. I had to put one foot in front of the other to get to the top of that hill. Only those who have walked up that hill can appreciate what I'm talking about! It is no small feat!

My younger years were so peaceful. I remember the sounds of our very quiet home. I would be sitting doing homework. I could see the reflection of the sun on the sea. Dad would be quietly snoring in his lazy boy recliner. Mom was gently rustling the pages of her newspaper that she would read every day.   The grandfather clock was ticking. I could hear the sound of the train going by on the tracks below. Yes, my young life was very, very happy.   I was surrounded with unconditional love and acceptance.

We do have a crazy family.   We laugh a lot. We are quite reserved and keep to ourselves, but we sure are funny. We had great holidays growing up, camping and water skiing at Osoyoos, driving to California, fishing at Loon Lake, and flying to Hawaii. And when we couldn't travel somewhere, my brothers would put me in a cardboard box that the groceries came home in and would push me all around the house in it.   We had so much fun and lots of "warm fuzzies."   I was pretty much allowed to run free and go and do whatever I wanted, and I was very happy.

I remember clearly lying in bed at night and wondering why I had been born, what was the real purpose of my life, and what was I supposed to be doing with it? Why was I born into THIS family and into THIS body?   My parents always took us to church when I was younger, and I had a godly Sunday School teacher who taught me the Bible. I was very aware of spiritual things, and would say I was searching for God.   At the age of six, a school friend invited me to an after-school meeting for children, where a Reverend Funk was clearly sharing the gospel of Jesus Christ with the use of clever magic tricks.   I knew I was a sinner and that I needed a Saviour. I prayed to receive Christ that day behind a fir tree in my backyard. I believe that my Sunday School teacher's good teaching had prepared my heart. I knew that it was the truth as soon as I heard it. I immediately knew that I would never be alone again, and I began praying to God about even the tiniest things.

When I put my trust in Jesus Christ, He put me on the purposeful path that I had been looking for. When significant things happened in my life, I knew that God had a purpose and a plan for me, and that I needed to pay attention!

I remember wanting the other children on my street to experience the love of God like I had, so I started a little "Christian Club" in our ironing room at home in the basement.   We had a Bible story, craft and sang a song. It is one of my first memories of being intentional.   Define intentional, you say?

It's doing something ON PURPOSE, hoping to achieve a desired result.

Chapter, the Second.

Learning to be Intentional.

"I can do all things through Christ Who strengthens me." *(Philippians 4:13 NKJV)*

I was blessed with parents who supported and encouraged me in EVERYTHING. In fact, the long list of intentional people who poured into my life giving wisdom, kindness, truth, musical ability, passion for life and love, is really quite astounding. I truly believe that the reason I have been able to live with so much intention is because of all the people who modelled this kind of life and passion for me. People were very purposeful about coming alongside of me to mentor and encourage me. How can I do any less for others?

My parents always taught me that I could do anything I set my mind to, and that nothing should ever stop me from achieving my biggest dreams. So, I boldly stepped into the "ADVENTURE," and have tried to spend time on things that really matter.

As I grew, I continued to love this world of "the music in my head" and learned to sing harmonies by studying how others did it so well. If I wasn't making or creating music, I was listening intently to it.

When I was six, I knew I wanted to play the piano and started praying for one of my very own. I saved pennies in a piggy bank for the piano I would one day own, and in the meantime I played my friends' pianos every time they offered. When I was 15, my parents purchased a piano, and I threw myself into it, heart and soul. By the age of 16, I was playing for the local Sunday School. By the age of 19, I was playing for weddings. Not because I was amazing, but just because I was WILLING. When friends asked me I would say, "YES!" I'll never forget playing for my friend's wedding. Someone told me afterwards that the bride had to just about run down the aisle because I was playing so fast. Yes, I was inexperienced, but willing.

I learned young that if the Lord asked me to do anything, I should always say "Yes, Lord" to Him, and trust that He would help me to do whatever He was asking me to do. When I was still a preteen, I continued to run the Bible Study Christian Club in the ironing room in our basement at home. I didn't know much, but I knew that people needed to hear about Jesus. There was a time when I decided to go to church on my own, wanting to learn the Bible and wanting to be around Christian people who loved me and encouraged me. I was literally there every time the doors were open. Those lovely people made me feel necessary, and gave me useful work to do, so that I felt needed. Those dear saints loved me, prayed for me, and guided me through my teenage years. The question placed to me was, "When is the time to serve God?" And the answer was simple. Today. Always today.

Our lives are so full of choices. Should I wear the red socks or the blue socks? Should I make pasta or rice? Should I have a Caramel Macchiato or a Ginger Tea Latte? There are so many opportunities in this world. Should I teach or should I go into retail? Should I be a professional musician or should I get into the catering business? There are also endless amounts of areas to study, things to learn, and copious experiences to try and to savour. It would be impossible in one lifetime to taste every opportunity and to learn everything there is to learn. With this in mind, I like to ask myself the question, if I had **only one week to live**, what would I spend my days doing?   The key here is to ask GOD what He wants me to be doing, right here and right NOW.

In my early years, I exposed myself to all manner of reading, which exposed me to the world around me. I have my mother to thank for this. Deeply ingrained in me is a passion for the written word and for books of all genres. I love fiction and nonfiction alike, and discovered early that books brought the world to my doorstep!

There have been wonderful people all along the way who put a passion in my heart for various pursuits. Camp counsellors who gave me a love for the Word of God, French and Social Studies teachers who gave me a passion to know more of the world, sewing and cooking teachers who taught me many practical skills, music teachers who gave me opportunities to write and arrange music for whole bands, and a clarinet teacher who spent hours with my friend Dawn and I to perfect our clarinet skills in order that we might be the best we could be!   My extended family, in Edmonton, Alberta was also extremely supportive of my spiritual life, always encouraging me to pray and to follow the Lord continually. I was baptized at the age of 18. My entire family attended as well as lots of my friends. I gave my testimony of God's faithfulness and it was definitely a life highlight! I stood in front of all who knew me and declared that I had given my life to Christ and that my intention was to serve Him, for the rest of my life!

When I finished high school, I really was hoping to go to the University of British Columbia to study music and be first clarinet in the Vancouver Symphony Orchestra. The Lord had other plans for me. My godly pastor and mentor, Ron Lovett, strongly suggested that I attend Peace River Bible Institute in northern Alberta, Canada. He had been a professor there, and highly recommended the Bible and Music Education Program, advising that it would prepare me for a life of ministry and usefulness. Following his advice, I spent three wonderful years there. God used so many people there to prepare me for the life I have since lived. Music, ministry, Bible, and people skills were all excellently taught and modelled for those of us who had the privilege of being students. Traveling on tour with a music team was a practical part of every year. We travelled throughout western Canada to take services, and I LOVED every minute of it.

Upon graduation, I realized that I did not want to be a Minister of Music at a local church, and decided to go to North West Baptist and Theological College, (NBTC) in Vancouver, to attain my Preschool Teaching Certificate. The program was excellent and I was well trained to teach in a preschool, and knew that I could get a job anywhere as a teacher if I so chose. During my time at NBTC, I had the privilege of singing in the school choir and going on tour with them as well to churches in the Vancouver area, as well as across Vancouver Island.

Around this time, I received a call from Don Klaassen, then a missionary with Global Outreach Mission, asking me if I would consider being on a yearlong, gospel ministry team that would travel across the US and Canada, and then to India. I knew immediately that it was TIME and said an excited "YES" down the phone to Don! I'll talk more about this later, but during this time I was so conscious of God's Hand in my life, and how He seriously had a plan for me. All I had to do was follow Him.

My husband has since said, "We should always be ready to speak, pray or die at any moment." I have added "sing or play" to that list. Literally, we can do anything that God is calling us to do, because He will always give us the skills and ability to do whatever He asks of us. We should take a NO FEAR approach and go for it! God is there to guide and help.

The Bible says we can do ALL things through
Christ, Who gives us strength.
(Philippians 4:13, my paraphrase)
We can, because He can!

So why is it important to learn to be intentional? I remember something that happened in 2001. Our family was driving to a friend's home in inner city London. Our youngest daughter, Heather, piped up to say, "Mummy, please remind Daddy to remember to stop when we get where we are going!" She did not want to miss the opportunities that visiting our friend's home would offer. And I do not want to miss anything that God has for me in this life either.

Some helpful questions I routinely ask myself about **my life**, **my conversations** and **my activities** are below.

Think of a specific topic or activity that is a part of your life at the moment and write it down here.

_____

_____

Will this matter 10 years from now? _____

_____

_____

Is this something I want to be remembered for? ____

_____

_____

When I get to the end of life on this earth, will I be thankful that I spent each day like I did? _____

_____

_____

_____

Take a moment to ask yourself these questions. If the answer to any of these questions is "No", then it's time to re-evaluate.

We need to make sure that our life goals match up with our day-to-day living.

Chapter, the Third.

Stop Drifting.

About being pursued.

My husband, Wyatt, and I had both been pursued and recruited to join the "Priority Team" that Global Outreach Mission (a ministry headquartered in Buffalo, NY) was going to send to colleges in North America to encourage student involvement in missions. We would then be sent to India for four months, and then spend one month in England before our return to Canada.   Wyatt was to be the team leader and speaker, and I was responsible for planning the programs and leading the music ministry. I was recruited from British Columbia, in Canada, and he was recruited from Mississippi. Wyatt was a great team leader. As the months of travel progressed, he proved to be a wise and gentle person, an honest critic, and a faithful encourager. He was fast becoming my best friend.

It never occurred to us, whilst we were working together, that our relationship would ever become more than a friendship, because at the time I was 22 years old and he was 35. We equally divided all of our time between every team member, and all of our relationships on the team were very healthy.

One day, Wyatt arranged to hold a team meeting on the rooftop of William Carey Baptist Church, in Calcutta, India. Everyone else was ill that evening, and only he and I showed up. Dare I say that there is no more beautiful night sky than an Indian one? After our abbreviated meeting, I went back down to my room in the residence. A Muslim girl, who had recently converted to Christianity, was sitting on my bed. She had, just that week, married a young Christian man, and they were hiding out in the church from her family who were pursuing her to put her to death. For their safety I will not mention their names, although I remember them as if it were yesterday. All I need to say is that she was pontificating on the advantages and blessings of being married to an older man. All of us who shared that room giggled like school girls, and in that moment I knew who I was going to marry. The adventure had begun!

I must say that my patience does me great credit. It took Wyatt a very long time to hear the same message that I had heard. The very night that the girls all sat in my room upon my bed talking about marriage, something else significant happened. The boys on our team bunked down in the church building, whilst we slept in the church's manse. That night, Wyatt was awakened with a dream. In his dream he knew that he was free to marry. But he was not told to whom. Thus begins my story of patience. He could not intentionally pursue me if he did not know WHO he was supposed to pursue!!

I tried to give him clues along the way which might indicate my feelings towards him, but evidently it was not TIME yet for him to know. We had a puppet stage on the platform every time we did a meeting. On one particular occasion we had an audience of several thousand people, row upon row of them, in the open air. When we were not speaking or performing, we gathered behind the puppet stage. Often we would pray fervently behind it, asking God to bless His Word, and to bring many people to faith in Christ. This one particular time, I remember that I was not praying. Instead, I kissed Wyatt on the cheek, told him I loved him, and then slipped out to sing the next song. I only hoped that it would start him to thinking!

When we left India, we did several weeks of mission in England, before returning to Canada. There was a day when I was very, very ill with fever and flu symptoms. I was in a serious state of delirium, and Wyatt came into my room, as the team leader, to see if I was all right. He put his lips to my forehead, which was evidently a method his mother had used, back in Mississippi, when he was a child, to test for fever. In my feverish state of illness, I truly thought this was a sign of his genuine concern and very deep love for me. This was back in 1984, when doctors in England still made house calls. He called the doctor in, and soon I was on the road to recovery, but I now believed him to be in love with me. It was another 8 long months before he would ask me to marry him. I have a very fickle heart sometimes, and in his wisdom, he recognized this, and wanted to wait and make sure that I knew what I wanted! He only proposed after I had been to his beloved home state, and knew what I was getting myself into. And then, because of the separation of 2,700 miles, he in Mississippi and I in British Columbia, he asked me to marry him over the telephone in December 1984. It was four months until we had an opportunity to see one another again.

Wyatt knew that the Lord had called him to minister in the country of England.   He had been for a summer mission trip, to Essex, in the summer of 1982, and felt called to do what he could to bring the message of the gospel back to the Island. At one time, this great country had sent so many missionaries to other lands, but this was now only history. The country that once sent so many missionaries around the world was now ripe to receive missionaries themselves.   A few gathered friends, around a kitchen table, began to plan, organize and finally register as a Charitable Trust, and in 1984, Emmanuel and Associates, Incorporated was born.   Later we would create charitable trusts in Canada and Great Britain, but this exciting part of our adventure had begun!

About pursuing.

There are countless numbers of people in this world who just drift. We believe that we are stuck in the job, home, situation, or relationship that we are in today. We seem to think that we have no control over improving our station or circumstances. But, what happens when we just let life carry us along?

Well, some of us might be very lucky, to meet the right people, get that dream job, or get to become rich, famous and good looking! Others of us, who just let life carry us along, might actually find ourselves in very despairing and desperate situations. In both cases, we might be asking ourselves, how did I EVER get to this place in my life? Often if we find ourselves in desperate situations, we may be blaming others. If we find ourselves in prosperous circumstances, we will often give ourselves credit. (Oh the fickleness of the human nature!)

God pursues us always. People pursue us sometimes. Sometimes we pursue God. Sometimes we pursue other people. Notice the exception in the four statements above? God ALWAYS pursues us. Intentionally. We can count on it.

If I could have been anything in my life, and it was just up to me, I would have been a professional musician. Why not? I'm as good as a lot of people out there, and better than some. But you see, I put myself in God's care, and His plan was better. Honestly. God's dreams for me are so much bigger than MY dreams for me.   And the same is true for you.

The Bible says that "in his heart a man plans his course, but the Lord determines his steps".
(Proverbs 16:9 NIV)

Does He want us to make plans? Absolutely. Does He want us to actively pursue His will for us? Yes. Does He have the right to change our plans? Of course! Sometimes as we make plans, He is getting us into position for whatever it is He has for us, or perhaps for something that we need to learn.   So don't just let life carry you along. Make those plans, but when you make them, give them back to God, because He really does know what's best for you.

Remember, God pursues us always.   He will not fail to notice a single step that you take!

Do I constantly and intentionally pursue God like He pursues me?   None of us do, although I know that my desire is to be that person who follows Him wholeheartedly. But we get distracted. I'm so glad that He is always pursuing me.   When I realize that I am THAT loved, it makes me want to turn and run into His open arms.

As soon as I was saved, I knew that my life had purpose. I knew I wanted to follow Christ, but of course, I did not know what that would mean. I DID understand that I wanted to KNOW Christ. That my life effort needed to be about pursuing Him.

"He must increase and I must decrease" is the verse that expresses my lifelong passion.
(John 3:30 KJV)

We can all think of examples of pursuing things or people. I remember when a portable library van used to stop at my street every Saturday morning. The librarian was diligently searching, all across London, for a certain book that I wanted to read. I remember mission recruiter Don Klaassen pursuing me every year, in hopes that I would sign up with Global Outreach Mission. Traveling around Bible colleges all over the US and Canada was another way that we pursued people to get involved in missions. We pursued people, not because of what we would get out of it, but because we knew that their lives would be changed if they got involved! We went to the dean of women at our Bible College one year, and asked if we might have access to the auditorium for holding nights of fasting and prayer.

We wanted to be intentional and diligent about seeking God, and pursuing Him! Those were incredible nights of singing, praying and crying out to God for the needs that we were aware of in the lives of people around us.

A man pursues a woman, with intention, when he wants to get to know her.   My husband is a perfect example of this. He was looking for a woman who loved the Lord more than she loved him.   If this woman could not be found, he declared that he would be happy to remain single the rest of his life.

People, think about what we spend our lives on! In my opinion, we spend far too much time valuing all the wrong things.   Our Christianity is laissez-faire, and we get caught up in what other people, our culture, or commercials on television tell us we should value!   Let's love history and <u>learn from it</u>. Americans are the first to say that they are going the way of Europe, as far as Christian values go.   It's time to be intentional.   We can make a difference!

As long as we are on this earth, we are never going to be done.   Serving.   Loving.   Teaching. Helping.   We need to keep being a 'Barnabus' to others.   In Acts 4:36,37 we read about the Barnabus who came along side of the apostle Paul to minister to him and to encourage him. I want to be that person.

It isn't over until the Fat Lady sings. And experiencing life on this earth doesn't end until we get to Heaven. I often reflect on some dear friends of Wyatt and I, Hamish and Margot McRae. They believed that they were called to offer hospitality to all believers. They believed that they were to encourage the brothers and sisters in the faith, and with joy. They lived by their beliefs. When we first went to England, they took us in and befriended us. They saw us as friendless strangers, and opened their home to us. Margot lived this way with her whole heart until she went to be with the Lord in 2015. Hamish is still faithfully ministering the Word of God whenever he has an opportunity, whether it be to one person, or 500. I also want to live this way to the end. I pray that God, Who is the One who fills my life with purpose and meaning, will help me to do this until my days on this earth are over.

No more drifting - stop it!

Let's stop valuing all the wrong things and start pursuing the best things.

If you want to make this really practical right now, stop and list some things below that you know to be the BEST THINGS.   Pursue these best things.

_____

_____

_____

_____

_____

_____

_____

_____

_____

_____

_____

_____

_____

_____

_____

Chapter, the Fourth.

Our call to the UK.

Pray and keep praying, all the time

and about everything.

(My favourite thing to say. VHG)

It was 1985. We were married.   The verse that we chose for our marriage was a prayer.

"May the beauty of the Lord our God be upon
us." *(Psalm 90:17 - KJV)*

It was printed on banners, and everyone present was there to see us commit to that, and also to hold us accountable in the days and years to come.

Would His beauty be seen in our lives? "O Lord, let it be so," was on our lips.

Wyatt & I had already been on short term mission trips. Emmanuel and Associates had been established as a non-profit organization in the United States. We knew we wanted to serve God full-time in Great Britain. We knew we were called by God to go to England. A car had been given to the ministry and was waiting for us in the United Kingdom, for our express use, as soon as we landed there. The only question was the timing of it all. When should we go?

We had been traveling and speaking at churches for the first year of our marriage, as well as volunteering at a local church in Jackson, Mississippi. We met with the Board of Emmanuel and Associates in August of 1986. They discussed the timing of our travel, and the fact that we were not yet fully supported. Someone said, "Well, what does Vicki think? Let's ask her." I took a deep breath. I swallowed hard and I said, "I think it's time to go now. There's no reason to wait. God will take care of us." Within a month we were landing at Heathrow airport, armed with a few suitcases and a whole lot of faith, believing that our God was going to show us what to do next.

At this point, in my story, I have to say that my husband is positively inspirational. He is full of faith, and believes that it is always too soon to give up. We rented a simple room in Hertfordshire, and began making ourselves more familiar with that part of the country and met as many people as we could. We went to the local church and had lunch with the pastor and his wife there. This church was also the fellowship that Hamish and Margot attended. We began to work with the young adults and did everything we could to get involved in people's lives. We travelled to see people who we had met previously on other trips, to scout out the land, and see where there might be opportunities to serve. We did not yet know what to do, only that we were to be there. We were willing to do anything that God put before us.

After a month of having only one room for a residence, we began to look elsewhere. We found a lovely pool house – literally a small dwelling on the side of a swimming pool – which had a small kitchen and a main room with a fireplace. This was a great improvement to the one room where we had been staying. Not having any space to turn around in, without bumping the other person was wearing a little thin. The pool house was on a gorgeous farm, in the village of Little Easton, in Essex. Over the next three years we would stay on this farm, although we did move twice, on the farm, into slightly largely accommodation both times. The farm was beautiful and such an amazing place to begin to plant our roots and to begin our new life. We made lots of friends, opened our home constantly for hospitality to others, and it became the place on the Island that we would continually return to, even to this present day. We would take long walks through the village. We prayed constantly that the Lord would open up more doors of opportunity for us. He did.

Wyatt preached a lot. I worked with a godly older man, Ron Hills, in several after-school Bible clubs. Ron was able to obtain access to pubs or church halls and the children would come weekly to hear the gospel stories and songs. He was a man of faith and it was a privilege for Wyatt and I to work with he and his dear wife. I remember there were three little old ladies and one gentleman keeping the door of the church in the village open, where we held one of the clubs. They persevered, as long as they were able, knowing that if they gave up, that services in the village would terminate, and there would be no evangelical witness in that village.

They were full of faith and did not want to see that happen. I learned resilience from their hard work and tenacious hanging on to the promises of God.

In reaching out to many people, there were some discouragements. One American pastor told us to "go home" and that Americans were never successful in England. We were surprised by his candour, and then realized, that because God was calling us, we should not let anything or anyone discourage us. We knew that God could open doors that no man could close.

We are so thankful for those first friends we made. Friends who encouraged us, thanked us, graciously were patient with us, and humbly accepted all our weak and simple offerings. I'm sure we learned far more from them than they ever learned from us.

Wyatt & I spent six months traveling from the farm, to a charming little village made of beautiful yellow stone, in the Cotswolds, every weekend. There we worked with a church that had not had a pastor for 100 years. It was an incredible time of ministry and opportunity. We took Sunday Services, preached, sang, and hopefully encouraged that little band of believers. We did gospel outreach in the local village hall, and knocked on doors to meet the community.   Soon after we left, they were able to call and support a full-time pastor! So encouraging!

Just before this, we were presented with a decision. The little church in Lechlade called us to come and pastor them, the same week that we also received a call from a church in the borough of Fulham, in London.   I remember it like it was yesterday. We loved Lechlade and had grown very attached to the dear people there. But London?   The call tugged at our hearts.   We did what we always have done. We spent three days praying.   Praying separately, I might add. We did not necessarily want to influence one another. We imagined what it would be like to serve in London.   Then we would imagine what it would be like to close that door and say yes to the village in the Cotswold's.   At the end of three days, Wyatt asked me what I thought we were supposed to do.   Again, as I had done before, I gulped, took a deep breath and said, "Well, I don't want to live in the city, but I believe that's exactly what God is calling us to do."   Wyatt nodded his assent. He felt exactly the same way. It was time to move.

Our ideal country experience was coming to an end. The English countryside would forever be in our hearts, and we were thankful for every day that we had spent there. It was like being in language school in any other country. We had watched, learned, interacted and studied the culture in a way that we could never have done had we not been given so much time. A friend wisely told us that we had rested for the hard work that was to come. She had no idea how true that statement was.

On May 14th, 1989 Wyatt was inducted as the Pastor of the church in London. We were supposed to be there to help for a period of one year. We stayed for fifteen. It was glorious. It was wonderful. It was so hard. But people were saved. Many people were taught the Word of God there, and then left London for the "outer parts of the earth," and are teaching and ministering in other countries to this day. We used to say that the world came to London. It's so true. We had 22 nationalities in the little church of 130 people at one point. Now that's what heaven is going to look like, people!

One of Wyatt's amazing strengths is his ability to connect people for the work of the gospel, or for any work. The strength of his ministry has always been these amazing connections between people from all over the world. Instead of guarding his pulpit like a pit bull dog, he would invite godly and wise men to preach to the congregation. Yes, he preached often, but the variety that he brought to our local church was phenomenal. More about this, and the Body of Christ, later!

Our passion for ministry is simply to serve. To get dirty. To be intentional. To ask what is needed. And then to just serve. We ask God what we are supposed to be doing today. What are we called to do? Then just do that. Many times we haven't known if we would have enough money to pay the bills that month. There have been many times when we have had no savings. But what we have is far better. We have a great and very wonderful God who has promised to give us all that we need in Christ.

For those who ask us how we knew what we were supposed to be doing, we suggest that you:

Decide what you love. Write it down here.

_____

_____

_____

_____

Examine what you're good at. _____

_____

_____

Ask yourself what your life experiences have
prepared you to do. _____

_____

_____

_____

Ask what resources are available to you. _____

_____

_____

_____

Consider your spiritual gifts. _____

_____

_____

Ask, "With all this in mind, what is GOD calling me
to do?"_____

_____

_____

_____

_____

Now, friend.

Just go do it.

In the faith that God gives you.

Chapter, the Fifth.

The Highways and the Byways.

The master told the servant, "Go out into the
streets and the lanes and make the people come
in, so that my house may be full."
(Luke 14:23 – ISV)

When I was a child I remember this verse being
talked about. The preacher would say that we
needed to get out of our comfort zone and go into
the highways and byways to meet people, and to
bring them back to the Master, Jesus Christ. To my
surprise, there is no such translation of this verse
that actually says, "Highways and Byways."
Apparently the preacher was talking about streets,
lanes or hedges. I haven't lately encountered

anyone in a hedge, have you?   But we get the idea. We are to make an effort to go where we might not normally go, in order to meet people we might not normally meet, in order to invite them to meet our God.

This world is full of more places to go than one person could possibly have time, energy or money to visit. But it's fascinating that there are so many tongues, tribes, people groups, and that in light of this, we usually have the audacity to think that **we are normal**! What?   It just makes me laugh.

I'll never forget an experience I had, whilst we were traveling to various Bible colleges, taking chapels and encouraging the students to consider missions. We were preparing to go to India within the month, and had just had our immunizations that day. I became very ill and feverish. I still remember the vivid dreams and hallucinations I had during that night of the raging fever. In the dream, I was given a crushing passion for China and for the people of China. I remembering praying fervently for them, and asking the Lord to save even just one, that night. The next day, I was up and around, feeling much better. Wyatt told me that the previous night he had been introduced to a young man in the guy's dormitory. He was from mainland China. Wyatt shared the gospel with him and the boy was saved that night. I learned from this experience that God uses anything and everything to accomplish His will in the lives of people. He wastes nothing. And sometimes when we can't get to other places in the world, the Lord brings the world to us.

While still on mission with the *Priority Team*, (the name that Global Outreach Mission gave our evangelistic music and drama team) we spent a few nights at Moody Bible Institute in Chicago, Illinois. They used to have an incredible Friday night prayer meeting, at which they prayed specifically, every week, for the nations and peoples of the world. After one such meeting, I went back up to the dorm room that we girls were sharing for the night. Briefly, I was alone and on the 13th floor, overlooking a magnificent view of the great city of Chicago. That night my heart was broken for that city, and for every city, filled with people needing to hear about the love of Christ, and the Hope He offers them. I wrote a song that night – a prayer that God, in Christ, would reach out to the people of the city of Chicago and that somehow He would use us, and give us the privilege of taking His message to the world that was crying out for hope. I believe that God was showing me His heart that night.

Shortly after this experience in Chicago we travelled to India. We spent four months living and traveling there, living with an Indian family, and learning all that we could of the culture. We've stayed very close to our Indian family, so that our children were raised having adopted Indian grandparents. Our lives are so much richer because of our relationships with them. They taught us how to laugh at ourselves, and how to appreciate and incorporate storytelling into our everyday family times. A storytelling culture does not forget its rich history, as quickly as a western culture that does not often take time to share those stories. In India we could not only feel the spiritual battle, but we could see it. I remember the Hindu festivals that would sometimes keep us awake at night. I remember going into a temple and being able to feel and smell the evil that was present. I remember seeing a demon-possessed girl, who was on exhibit to show the greatness of the god they worshiped. And then I remember the peace and tranquillity of Mother Theresa's Home for the Destitute and Dying. Oh, the contrast! There I saw every person being treated with love and dignity, and the difference between the two extremes was unforgettable and life-changing. I remember noticing that it is only the love and power of God that changes lives, brings hope, and offers redemption.

After our time in India, we flew to Great Britain, where we spent one brief month doing ministry. Once married, we later returned and lived there permanently for twenty-three years. This was the powerful nation that had once sent missionaries to every corner of the earth. The history is still there, and I glory in it, wanting to remember all that God did with a people who were willing to follow Him. We had the privilege of living there permanently for 23 years. Our children were born there. We walked beside these resilient, funny, particular and sometimes peculiar people, and loved them. I can say to the English, as Paul said in his letter to the Philippians, "I have you in my heart." Even the names of the towns and villages that we lived in and near, cause me to feel warm all over – names such as Furneux Pelham, Sherborne, Bishop's Stortford, Little Easton, Thaxted, Bradwell, Lechlade, Fulham, Kingston upon Thames, Wimbledon, Finchingfield, Hammersmith, Putney, Great Dunmow, Chepstow, Monmouth, to name just a few. The charm and beauty of the place has captured my heart forever.

During our time in London, we lived in an old Victorian row house, that had retained its original Victorian floor tiles. Charm exuded from every nook, and in the glass above the front door the name "Glenisla," given to our home by a previous resident, was displayed. We have often heard the saying that an Englishman's house is his castle. Well, I learned not to get obsessed with my kingdom! We definitely shared our "castle" in London. I used to tell Wyatt that he could bring people home and I would feed them. This was a constant occurrence. I met many people only one time, fed them, and then would never see them again. We offered hospitality to those who were lonely, needy, visiting the city, and also church members and friends regularly. We believed the Scripture that says,

---

"An elder should be given to hospitality!"
(1 Timothy 3:2 - KJV)

Christmases' were particularly memorable, since most of our church people were occupied with their families. We would invite students in for Christmas day, such as the young man from mainland China who was in London for a short period of study. We spent one Christmas with our next door neighbour, Miss Winnifred Smith, who had been secretary to Winston Churchill during the War. Certainly I learned that when I was willing to line up my priorities with GOD'S WILL for me, that my life was always interesting and exciting!

Many people who have never strayed from the comforts of North America, cannot imagine the overwhelming sense of evil that is so obviously less veiled in other countries. I remember one night in London, waking up to an overwhelming sense of evil - an evil that had me in its grip. The woman who lived across the road from us had told us that she talked to demons, and although we talked to her about the Lord and were kind to her throughout the years, she remained very disturbed. That night, this woman was walking up and down the centre of the road, swearing and blaspheming. All I could do was say the Name of Jesus. I prayed when I was able to, and reminded the Lord that He had paid the price on the cross for all of my sin. My hope was in Him. I was trusting in Him. I got out of bed, kneeled on the floor beside it, and claimed the blood of the Lord Jesus Christ over this terrible battle that I was aware of. I prayed for the lady, Immelda, and asked that the Lord would quench the forces of evil and give her peace. She immediately stopped ranting and went back inside of her home. Never again did I doubt that there are evil forces all around us. And never again was I afraid. The Lord already won the victory when He rose again from the dead. Jesus Christ has conquered death and the grave!

We moved to Chepstow, in Wales in 2004.   My children had a castle to play in – a castle that William the Conqueror had started to build in 1667. We lived in a 200-year-old farmhouse with two kitchens, a servant's staircase and thick stone walls. We had ancient walnut and plum trees.   We walked the beautiful Wye Valley, and celebrated Christmas in the old Tintern Abbey by torchlight. We loved the openness and the humour of the Welsh people. Such kindness and friendships we met there!   Once in Wales I remember waking up with a paralyzing, unexplainable fear.   The enemy of my soul was trying to steal my joy, and I knew instantly what I had to do.

Ephesians 6:12 tells us that "our struggle is not against flesh and blood, but against the rulers, against the authorities, against the powers of this dark world and against the spiritual forces of evil in the heavenly realms." *(NIV)*

I learned from my time in India, as well as in London, that I only needed to claim the blood of Jesus, and cry out to Him.

I would like to address the spiritual temperature of the United Kingdom for a moment.   My simple experience has been to notice that a majority of the population does not even acknowledge that there is a God in Heaven. Certainly not a god that would desire a relationship with people that He had made! And in the many interviews that Wyatt conducted with people on the streets, over the years, he found that many do not even know the Name of Jesus. Individuality is an important quality, and individualism is valued. People believe that "when you're dead, you're dead." It reminds me of the familiar saying "Eat, drink, and be merry, for tomorrow you will die." This depiction of the philosophy of epicureanism is actually derived from two separate Bible passages. Ecclesiastes 8:15 talks about the comfort that eating and being glad are during a person's long life of work. 1 Corinthians 15:32 says that if the dead are not raised back to life then we might as well just eat and drink, because tomorrow we may die! In other words, "what's the point?" and that is the view of many in Great Britain and Europe today.

Why am I dwelling on the spiritual battle that we experienced again and again? Because this spiritual battle, that takes place in the heavenly places, is often veiled in North America and other prosperous, western cultures. Just because we cannot see it or feel it, does not mean that it does not exist. We need to put on the full armour of God (Ephesians 6:13 NIV) and trust ourselves into His care.

We moved to the United States in 2008. My husband wanted our children to experience American culture. They were growing up quickly, and while they were still living in our home, we wanted them to experience yet again another culture. While all four of them possess three citizenships (British, Canadian, and American), they had only visited North America for short vacations.

Let me say a few things about Canada first. I grew up there. The majestic beauty that is to be seen everywhere is comparable only to places like Switzerland and Germany, in my humble opinion. Canadians are known, all over the world, for being nice. It's true. The people in Canada are down-to-earth, and it's a slower pace of life. Not because they don't work hard. Oh no. Canadians work very hard, but they know how to play hard too. They do their work well, and then they play well. As an adult, looking back on the culture that I was raised in, I have to admire it deeply. There is none of this "all work and no play" business.

Canadians pride themselves for being tolerant of other cultures and religions. Acceptance of the wishes of others is hugely important. It's all about being a good person. You may disagree with me, but there seems to be a huge apathy about God. People just don't want to know.

My impressions of the United States? People value teamwork, freedom and the American dream. The spiritual battle is more veiled here. There are churches on every street corner, but little passion in the hearts of God's people. The church doesn't seem to know how to really sing to God. One great thing is that many young people are being brought up by parents who teach them the Word of God, or at least take them to church so that someone else can. When we moved to the United States, my children, for the first time, had a choice of which Christian children to become friends with. They were no longer so isolated, and had peers they could connect with who believed similar things to what they had always been taught. My children did comment that our new-to-us, seven-year-old house had no personality. Certainly it had little history to speak of. And we felt quite lonely when we moved to the United States. People drive everywhere and you may live in a nice house, in a nice neighbourhood, but your neighbours may want to keep very much to themselves.

I guess I always imagined, that when I sat down to write my first book, I would be sitting in an English garden, sipping tea, listening to the birds chirping, with a dog by my feet, and typing on a manual typewriter. Nothing is farther from the truth. I am sitting in an air-conditioned home, in the state of Georgia, in the US. It is 95 degrees Fahrenheit outside. My dog has died and I can't find my old typewriter. Well, this will have to do.

Why did I want to write about the "highways and byways?" Because I have learned that I need to value what God values. That nothing should be too much trouble, and that if God has called me to do something, then I'd better go and do it! If I make excuses I will be miserable. "Ready and willing," needs to be my motto. If God has called me to do something, then He will provide a way for me to do it. If I don't see any opportunity yet to do what He is calling me to do, then I need to pray and ask God to open a door of opportunity. He may even want me to create that opportunity!

It is a faithful saying, that if I spend my life giving to others, then God will meet every need that I have.

No exceptions.

Chapter, the Sixth.

A passion for People.

"they will be called . . . a planting of the Lord **for the display of His splendour**." *(Isaiah 61:3 – NIV)*

Understanding people.   Wow, if you get to the place where you have figured people out, let me know okay? The variety and intricacies of people is simply too deep of a subject to fathom. People have designed all sorts of tests to help understand themselves and others. I find these sorts of tests really useful – tests such as the *Myers-Briggs* test, the love language categories and the Temperament test. We are not meant to use these methods to label or judge other people, but I believe that if they help me understand the people that I live and work with just a little bit better, then they have accomplished their purpose.   I, for example, am an introverted extrovert. I love people and being with people, but I recharge my batteries by being alone. I also tested as 100% an Artist on the *Myers-Brigg* test. What is the usefulness of knowing this? Only that when I look at how my children, my husband, or my friends test, it helps me to work on my relationships with them by showing me how I can best communicate with each one effectively. I care a lot about communicating with people effectively, and if these tests help me to do that, then I will use them!

In grade three, I remember very clearly being assigned the role of the "Christmas Tree" in the school play. Seriously. They obviously thought I had no talent at all. I didn't even have one line. I just had to dress up in this hot, uncomfortable tree costume for the entire length of the Christmas Play. I do remember wanting to communicate well with others. I was just very shy and needed to learn that the important part was the message, not the messenger.   If someone you know is passionate about something, notice how fluent they can become when they talk about what they love. I remember standing on the cement stairs of the school gym at the elementary school I attended. It was recess, and I stood up there to sing a song I had written. My friend bravely stood with me, and was my backup singer. I was passionate about this song, so any shyness I felt faded into the background, at the opportunity of sharing this song that I loved.

I truly believe that God wants us to be passionate about people. My husband is passionate about the souls of people and I have learned so much from him. Where ever we have lived, we have made it our goal to get to know the names of all of the people on our street. We would pray for our neighbours, and have prayed Scripture over each family, for example, the Lord's Prayer. We might pray,

"Lord, may your will be done in the Smith family today. Please provide every need that they have. May they lift up Your Name. May Your Kingdom come in their lives today. May they learn to understand Your forgiveness and forgive others who have trespassed against them. May they desire to know You and give You the glory that You deserve."

As we began to pray the Lord's prayer for the families on our street, an interesting phenomenon started to happen. Instead of crossing the street so they would not have to speak to us, they would look us in the eyes and say hello. Apathy was replaced with caring. I remember the day that a man named Jivad knocked on our door, and asked if we could help him change a light bulb. Walls were broken down, and it was the very specific and personal prayers that had done it!

Every Christmas we would buy enough poinsettias for every family on our street. That was a lot in London. We would write a card that said something like, "Merry Christmas from the Gwin family at Number 26," and take them door to door. One woman said that she had lived on that street for 15 years, and no one had ever before given her a gift at Christmas. We knew that it was important to pray for the specific needs of people, and how could we do that properly if we didn't even know their names!? After we got to know them a little, we would have barbeques or parties that we could invite them to. I was always so surprised at how many would come. Perhaps, just the novelty of seeing how someone else lived was a draw. Certainly there are many lonely people all around us, who would never articulate their own need to us, but would come to a social gathering. Often, once people see that we had a very alive and real faith in God, they would open up about their own lives and ask us to pray for them. Over the years, so many have come to us, requesting prayer, when they didn't have a relationship with the Lord themselves, and would say that they didn't know how to pray.

Do you remember the popular course in the 1990's called *Experiencing God*? In that book, the author, Henry Blackaby, instructed us to see where God is already at work, and join Him there. This was profoundly life changing for me. To understand, that even when I cannot see it, God IS at work. I needed to pay attention.

I believe that God divinely appoints places for us to be, and people for us to be around. If I'm aware of this, and looking for ways to initiate conversations with people, amazing things can happen every day. I need to realize that the person sitting across the room from me at the coffee shop may be experiencing a real spiritual battle, and that Satan does not want her to have a relationship with Christ. I am learning to pray, while I drink my coffee, asking God to show me when to speak. I may not have the gift of evangelism, but I can care about people.

I can open my mouth, put myself in situations where I am vulnerable, so that I will have to trust God. If I trust God, He will use the gifts He has given me to lead others to Him.

I so want my life to be a display of God's Splendour, for His Glory!

A man named Robert lived at the end of our road. Outside on the sidewalk. He had a shopping trolley that I suppose he had taken from a grocery store, and in it were all of his earthly possessions. Sometimes he would put his boom box on someone's stone wall, in front of someone's house so he could have music to listen to. Other times he would line up all of his beer bottles on that same wall. The local shop would give him day old sandwiches and other food, that they could no longer sell because of the expiration date on the packages. Our family walked a great deal in London. Traffic was bad, and walking was good for us. Very nearly every day we would have to walk past Robert, on our way to the library, the park, the church, or the shops. My sweet Elizabeth, then about three years old, had so much compassion for our local homeless person. One day she asked me if she could offer him a banana as she passed by. I don't remember if he accepted it or not, but I do remember his smile and the warmth that he expressed at Elizabeth's kindness. The saddest day of all was the day that our family came home from church in our van, only to see the dustmen (garbage collectors) picking up Robert's shopping trolley, and throwing it into the truck, as if it didn't matter to anyone. The teddy bear, the boom box, the food, the blankets, were all gone. Robert was told to move on and we were devastated for him.

I will sum up my thoughts here and say with Meg Ryan (in the movie, *You've Got Mail*) – "Whatever else it is, it should START by being PERSONAL!" Every person matters.

Yes, the smelly bag lady, who used to come into the church building on a Sunday, because she wanted to sit in the warm room for an hour and have a cup of tea. She matters to God so she needs to matter to me.

My youngest, most outgoing child taught me a valuable lesson one day. She was only 17 months old, and did not do quiet time in her room well. She would throw every toy out of her crib and then just cry. She wanted real people around her. The only occasion that I remember her being really happy in room time, was the day we heard her yelling, "hallo, hallo!" at the top of her voice. She could reach the window curtain from her crib and had pulled it aside to look out. The Irish lady, who lived across the road, used to lean out of her upstairs window for hours at a time every day, when the weather was fine. My Heather was connecting with this unusual, unlovable woman. She was personally connecting with her by waving wildly and calling out to her. I don't think we can underestimate the importance of a personal connection with other people.

Once when I was extremely ill (more about this later), I had to be pushed in a wheelchair at the airport, so that I could make a needed trip back to North America, to see my family. I will never ever forget the experience. As I was sitting in the chair, and being pushed, not one person looked at my face or into my eyes. They talked to the aid who was pushing me and caring for me, but it was as if I did not exist. I was not there. I made a resolution that day to care for the people I meet who sit in those chairs, many of whom may spend hours every day indoors, and alone, with no human contact. I want to notice them and say a kind word. It's such a little thing.

I guess what I'm saying, is that I want to choose to be intentional about my relationships with others. Not just my family, or my friends, or people I have been introduced to, but everyone God puts into my path today. I believe I can make a difference. I may not be able to change the lives of millions of suffering people in this world today, but I can start with one person. If it matters to God, I believe it needs to matter to me.

I remember the day that I tidied up the guest room in my farmhouse. I wanted a quiet sanctuary to come to and to be alone with God. You know, like the prayer closet in the *War Room* movie. I wanted to be free from distractions. The peacefulness of the room, and the prayerfulness of it, also must have appealed to my cat, for I was never alone in there. I wonder if, just as cats can sense our demeanour and calm aspect, that people can too, and will want to be with us? This was a reminder to me, to never underestimate the encouragement that we might be to one person who needs it today. I want to be passionate about encouraging people. I remember back in Bible College, that the staff provided "Encouragement Cards" for the students. There were many days when I came to my mailbox, tired and discouraged, only to find that someone had written an encouraging word, or a Bible verse, that was just exactly what I needed at that moment. It taught me that when the quiet voice of the Holy Spirit, puts another human being on my heart, that there is a reason, and that I should act on it.

I have heard that a common Alcoholics Anonymous quote is, "We are not all sick on the same day." Isn't that great?   When I'm discouraged, someone around me may be encouraged and able to minister to me, and visa-versa. Hebrews 13:6 tells us to not forget to do good and to share with others in need. God is pleased when we reach out to others!   And I don't think this is just talking about physical needs. People are so needy, aren't they?   You and I included!

I want to be interruptible.   As mentioned before, we do need to make plans, but if God wants to change our plans, shouldn't we be ok with that? I have seen God, so many times, when I thought that this was really the only time I had to do such and such a project, make time for me later, when I have been willing to set my plans aside, for the person that He brings across my path.   And about children, let me just add here that when they want or need to talk, it's okay to drop everything.   When you are given a window into your child's heart, take it! So many times my kids have come to sit on my bed at midnight, and if I had told them I was too tired to talk, I would have missed some of the most precious moments of my life.

On one day, in 2009, I realized that I could be kind, I could reach out to people, and I could try to explain the love of God to others, but that it wasn't enough. I realized that I needed to cry out to God, that He would have mercy on all of humanity, and bring people to a saving knowledge of Himself. Quoting from my journal,

"I am so aware of my helplessness – my hope is in God alone. When you realize that nothing you can say or do can make another person believe what you believe, or see things as clearly as you do, or embrace truth, then you are driven to your knees. In Ecclesiastes, King Solomon described a life without God as having no meaning. He said that life without God was all vanity, chasing after the wind, and meaningless. I can attest to the truth of that, and realize with all humility that only by His grace, have I seen and understood this. I'm a wretched, horrible sinner and any goodness in me points to Christ and Him alone. Oh Lord, have mercy on those you have created. I especially ask for those in my own family, that each one would seek after You.

Help us O Lord. Have mercy I pray. All the glory
will be Yours."

___

If you want to make a difference in the lives of the people around you, here are some questions you might ask.

When will I do good to others? _____

_____

Do I listen more than I talk? _____

_____

Am I prepared to speak truth when I have the opportunity? _____

_____

Am I willing to make that opportunity? _____

_____

What does God want me to do this week to reach out to someone? _____

_____

_____

_____

_____

_____

_____

_____

How can I be praying for the people who live, work or play around me?

_____

_____

_____

_____

Chapter, the Seventh.

The "What If" Syndrome.

The good, the bad and the ugly.

All of us have either said, or have heard someone say the words, "But what if . . . "
There will always be those of us who ask, "What if this had happened?" or "What if that had occurred?" I'd like to say that there are two ways to approach these questions. The first is dismal and can lead to despair. Let's call that the "bad and ugly" approach.

We have all made bad decisions. And all of us have been affected by the bad decisions of other people. These choices are history. They should be dealt with, accepted and let go. No matter how much we would like to change our history – it cannot be changed. It is now simply a factual record of what happened in history. We may not be proud of it, but it's done and over. Some things that fall into this category are:

1. Who I married

2. What college I went to

3. How I have spent my life up to this present minute.

There is no point in asking, "What if I had married someone else?" or "What if I had grown up on the other side of town, or in another country?" or even, "What if I had been born into a different family?" We need to just let these things go. We can learn from our mistakes, our environment and our experiences, but then we need to just let them go.

The other approach is life giving and totally inspiring for a full, happy and meaningful life. Let's call that the "good" approach.

These are the choices that actually help motivate us to greatness.

Let's ask ourselves questions like, "What if I crossed the street today, to reach out to my neighbour?"

"What if I decided to be less focused on work, and more focused on what really matters in this life?"

"What if I decide to volunteer at my local church?"

"What if I were to pack my suitcase to go across the world to reach others with the gospel of Jesus Christ?"

"What if I were to pay for the person's meal at the next table in the café?"

"What if I were brave and decided to write and publish my first book?"

What might happen, if I were to pay attention to my dreams, and be intentional about following the Lord, and His Amazing, Big, Oversized dreams for me?   Would my days count for something?   Would my financial needs be met?   Would my life be a useful, well spent life?

YES! YES!!!! And YES!!!!!!!!

I have made so many mistakes. I've done lots of things without being intentional in my life. But my heart, is to learn from the mistakes of others, as well as my own mistakes. Elisabeth Eliot said that "God never wastes anything". I sure don't want my painful mistakes to be wasted. I want to learn from them and not make the same mistakes twice, if at all possible!

How do we know what those good choices are? Well, when I don't know what to do, and seemingly have too much to do, I have learned to ask the Lord what I should do next. He seems to love that prayer, because as soon as I pray it, He guides my thoughts and orders my priorities. James told us that if anyone lacks wisdom, he should ask God for it. (James 1:5 - paraphrase mine)

He's just waiting for us to ask.

It's very interesting to me that before the Word of God came to Zechariah, that there was a 400-year silence. In Zechariah 7 it says that the people's hearts were hard and that they would not listen to God. So God stopped speaking. Oh, may my heart stay tender towards God, so that I will hear His voice in my life every day. I never want Him to stop speaking.

Sometimes, when He shows me what to do, I doubt my ability to do what He wants me to do. For instance, I'm terrified to walk across the street to take cookies to that neighbour who I think does not like me. I learned something wonderful in a Beth Moore Bible study years ago. When insecurity starts to make me doubt, I flip it around and say, "God I doubt myself, but I will not doubt YOU! I will let Your perfections override my feelings of imperfection. I will do what You instruct me to do."

It is time to stop thinking about ourselves. God has a much better plan for us than we could ever have for ourselves. It's time to trust Him.

Let's interact with this.

Think of anything in your past that you need to let go of. Pray and give it to God. _____

_____

_____

_____

_____

List here what you believe God is asking you to do. What can you do TODAY as a step towards this?

_____

_____

_____

_____

_____

_____

_____

_____

_____

Chapter, the Eighth.

Living Effectively

Outside of Your Culture.

In June 2000, my little Elizabeth ran into the kitchen. Her curls were bouncing and she was wearing a pretty, white, flowery dress. She exclaimed with her usual exuberance, "Mama, there's a bee in the living room and it thinks I'm a flower!"

She fit into the scene perfectly. She was imagining the scenario from the point of view of another living creature. Imagining that she was a flower, did not make her a flower, but in her mind, it did convince that bee that she was worth pursuing! That's kind of what living outside of your culture is like.

Eventually, people forgot that I was Canadian. I was one of them. At long last I became more at home in the UK than I still am in Canada or the USA. Today

I am English between my ears.   But it was not always so.

When we first moved to England, I purchased a small Collins dictionary to keep in my handbag.   No matter where we were, I would hear words that were outside of my vocabulary. I wanted to learn them, and be able to use them.   People in North America think that they can just move to Great Britain and acclimate immediately. Nothing could be farther from the truth. Local slang is different wherever you go, but it's so much more than that.   Vocal inflection, word order, word meaning and sentence structure are all tremendously different from what I was raised to speak. I remember marvelling at the little children in our after-school kid's clubs.   They not only had a wonderful ability to use the English language, but they had been taught to be sceptical, to question things and to inquire why!   When I was eight or nine years old, I never would have questioned an adult like these children questioned me.   I was very impressed that they were taught to think and wanted to learn!

People showed so much grace to me, while I was learning. I will never forget the time I invited a family over for tea. I served them hot tea and biscuits (cookies).   They stayed for an hour.   I served more tea and more biscuits. They stayed for another hour. Finally, I realized that they understood that they had been invited to dinner! I excused myself, went to the kitchen, and quickly made some sandwiches. It was only after the sandwiches, that they thanked us for the tea, and bid us farewell. That was one of life's embarrassing moments. We became friends with that family and laughed about that incident many, many times. Evidently, tea could be enjoying a meal together around 5 p.m. or it could be a cup of tea and a biscuit (cookie). Who knew?

We watched how people interacted with one another. They were not at all afraid of silence. Once we attended a Bible study in someone's home. They all sat quietly, appearing to be staring at their own shoes. A natural thing for any American to do, is to try to fill that silence with conversation. We found it very, very awkward to just sit, with people we had never met before.

At first, until I could speak the language without much of an accent, I would just stop speaking altogether. I got tired of being called "that Canadian girl," so I would not talk unless absolutely necessary.

The first thing we acclimated to, was the size of the small refrigerator. Our fridge in the pool house was the size you might see in a trailer, in Canada. You know the kind with the tiny freezer up on top. Because of this, we would go to the shops at least every second day, to get the things that we needed.

I remember once, going to a pastor's home. He and his wife had invited us for tea. This was in the 1980's when they would serve not only four different kinds of sandwiches, but four puddings (or dessert), as well. There was so much cheese and cream, and I think I gained 20 pounds in the first three months of living there! As I was taking a sandwich from the tray that they passed to me that day, they said, "Oh how lovely. You like tongue, do you?" (Literally the tongue of a cow, sliced thinly for sandwiches) I quickly murmured something about being delighted to have the opportunity to try it, and was stuck.

I would go to the Butcher's once a week, "Sweetlands" it was called, in Great Dunmow. They were so nice and remember me to this day. A British butcher will cut the meat exactly as you request it. There will often be cow tongues in the window, and rabbits, hanging outside to be purchased. A delicacy for my children at the butcher in Wales were the sugar mice on the counter. Yes, these adorable mice sweets were made out of sugar, and often with a little string tail. These were an absolute necessity if we were passing, and sometimes, we made a special trip!

What you have to understand about the British is that having a cup of tea is an event. It's not something you carry around with you, like an American carries a bottle of Coke in case he gets thirsty. It is an event. It makes everything better. And when you don't know what to do, you have a comforting cup of tea. When you don't know what to say, you ask someone if they would like a cup of tea. When you ask someone if they would like a cup of tea, they will usually say "no thank you." When you ask them a second time, they will ask you if YOU'RE going to have one. If you say "yes," then they may say, "Well, alright then, if you're having one," at which point you proceed to have a cup of tea together. If someone has stayed at your home for a very, very long time, and it's time for them to go, you ask them if they would like another cup of tea. At which point they stand up and say, "Oh no, but thank you very much. I really must be going."

While you were having your cup of tea, you no doubt exhausted the topic of the weather. It is absolutely astounding how long a British person can converse about the weather. What it was like yesterday. What it promises to be like tomorrow. And how many times it has changed in the last few hours. How silly I was to leave my umbrella at home, and how seldom the weather men are actually right. Sigh.

We've been talking about what it is like to live effectively in another culture. Let's now explore the benefits of bringing up children in another culture. Well, they realize that the world does not revolve around them, and that there are others ways of doing things. We often said to our kids, "This is the way we do it at our house," just to make a point that just because we think something is polite or correct or best, does not make it so. Children raised in other cultures are creative because of this. They think outside of the box. Often, as individuals, they are not as influenced by their culture and their peers. They really are okay with being different from the people who live around them. They learn to glory in the diversity of that experience.

Going to the doctor or hospital in another country was a huge learning curve for me. Medicine seems to be so different in every country, and you have to adjust to a new way of doing things. That pretty much sums up everything in a new culture. You keep your eyes and ears open to watch and to listen. It's all about learning and not trying to impose your way of doing things onto other people.

(This is an aside - I had all 4 of my babies at Queen Charlotte's Hospital in London. They closed it down when I was finished having babies. Ha ha.)

Learning to drive a standard shift was huge for me. You cannot drive a standard shift in the UK with an automatic license. And most people from North America drive an automatic car. I had to take my driving test all over again, so I took driving lessons, to learn the British road rules, as well as to learn to drive a standard shift. And YES, I passed on my very first try. I'm still very sentimental about my first car in England. It was a used Austen Maxi, circa 1972. Oh I loved that car. I would go on all the little one track back roads, through the countryside, glorying in the beauty and loving the freedom that that car gave me. We made friends who lived in several neighbouring villages, and I loved to visit them in their ancient cottages with their delightful gardens and pets. I learned more from them than they ever could have learned from me.

One very important thing Wyatt & I learned early on was how important it was to integrate fully into the culture. I remember one Sunday we travelled into London to visit the American church. The expats there may have been very happy, but I was so disappointed. It was like being back in the United States, and what is the point of being in another culture if you do not plan to learn from that culture and integrate! I liken this to the story of the missionary, Hudson Taylor, who went to China and became as Chinese as the most Chinese! That was my goal.

I am always very interested in how other people live. One day, my family may put this quote of mine on my tombstone, "I could live here!" I say it at least once a week. I used to love walking around the streets of Fulham, in London, at twilight. People had not yet shut their curtains for the evening, and you could hear music playing and people talking. You could see people setting the table for supper, sitting doing their homework, or perhaps just watching the tele. People are so interesting and we can learn so much from them!

The key thing about living effectively in another culture is realizing that you don't need to go in to show the locals how to "do things right." Humility is needed. To get to know people over the years, we involved ourselves in the community. Dog walking is a British national pastime. Did you know that? If you move to Britain and want to get to know people, then get a dog and go for a walk. It works every time. You would ask someone you met on the path what the name of their lovely dog was. Let's say it was "Lucy". The man walking the dog of course became Mr. Lucy. It was a fabulous introduction and a great way to meet people.

When you move to a new community, whether it be in a new city, a new state or a new country, see what is needed, and then do that. When we lived in Wales there were a group of believers wanting to start a church in an area without an evangelical church in the town. We came alongside of them and helped where we could. Once, when we were visiting a small lake resort in Canada, there were no services on a Sunday at the campground, so we held services on the Sundays that we happened to be there. Ask yourself, what do the locals need? Then do that!

It is very important to remain true to one's self, when living outside of your culture. Always be who God created you to be, and tell the truth about everything. No matter what culture you are in at the moment, God values truth and people always need to hear truth.   Keep the main thing, the main thing.   I am a sinner and I need a Saviour. Everyone else is a sinner and I need to show them grace and the Saviour.

The day we immigrated from our beloved UK was the 11 February 2008. We left the land of walking pavements, local village communities and neighbourhood pubs. We moved a cat, 4 children, a golden retriever and a 40-foot container of earthly possessions to the United States. The children had never before lived in the US and I had only lived there for one year, back when we were first married. It was a huge culture shock for us all. We were strangers in a strange land. After driving for 31 years in other places, I had to retake my driving test on American soil. I was a master at parallel parking from our many years in London, but failed my parking in the US because the steering wheel happened to be on the other side of the car. So many changes.   Here is an excerpt from my diary, that first year that we lived in the US as a family.

"Today was a FUNNY day – and it wasn't that I
laughed very much, either. After such a long time
here in the States, today I felt like a foreigner all over
again. When you have to ask questions about simple
things, people assume you know nothing at all about
those things, when really, you may even have more
experience and knowledge than they do, but they
just use different words to express it. And because
you have to ask, they assume you know nothing. Oh
well, a lesson in humility, right?"

This is quite disjointed, but that's how you feel when
you happen to forget what country you're in, what
vernacular to use, and how to best communicate
with the person who is sharing your space right
now.

How can one live effectively outside of their culture?
Have a teachable spirit, learn how to laugh at
yourself and keep trying.

It's always too soon to give up.

I would ask myself, "When is the time to serve God?"
And the answer was simple. Today. Always today.

Chapter, the Ninth.

Just. So. Sick.

"Oh awesome Gentle Saviour.

Shed Your Light upon my path.

Let me know You walk beside me

Till You bring me Home at last."

(For Being There by VHG)

There was a day in my life when the unthinkable happened. It was September 12, 1994. I had a four-year-old, a two-year-old, and a two-month old baby. I sat down in the king wicker cane chair in my kitchen, and said, "I can't do another thing until you take me to the doctor." My wise husband looked at me, took me seriously, and proceeded to call in a friend to look after the children. He drove me to the doctor's office and we waited until someone had the time to see me. I remember not even being able to sit upright in a chair. I was told by the doctor that I had a 72-hour viral chest infection. I needed to go home, have complete bed rest, and I would be fine. We took her seriously. Bed rest. Someone helped with the children. I did not get better. My chest felt like it had 24 bricks sitting squarely on it, my skin tingled all over, and my muscles ached. The light in the bedroom gave me an intense headache, and within days I was enclosed in a dark room, could hardly walk, did not have the strength to dress and undress myself, the energy to speak, or the will to feed myself. I must say here that I was NOT depressed.

My husband got help for me. Missionary nannies came who could look after the house and the children so that I could recover (he said in faith). No one had been able to say what was really wrong with me. I still did not have the strength to sit upright. After six months of being this ill, a Christian doctor in London, England who had just been taking courses on the subject of Chronic Fatigue Syndrome got up from his desk, walked over to me, kissed my cheek gently, and said with compassion, "I am so sorry to tell you this, but I believe you have Chronic Fatigue Syndrome."

I looked at him incredulously while he hastened to explain that there were rare instances, when people get a viral illness, and instead of it going away after the 72 hour expected period, the virus does not go away. It starts to wreak havoc in the person's body by beginning to destroy brain cells. The outcome of that, he explained, was that a person continued to feel as if they were very, very ill, but when their vital signs were checked, literally nothing amiss would show up in any medical tests that were done. In England there is a medical term for this called Myalgic Encephalomyelitis, or M.E. Some people recover, but many do not.

I eagerly began to do whatever the doctor's told me to do, wanting to be that "good" patient, who was trying hard to work with them while they clutched at straws. Finally, after several years, they passed me over to a recovery specialist (perhaps she was a psychologist under a different name) and we worked hard to get me to the best quality of life that was going to be possible for me. I remember her telling me that I WAS the patient who was going to get well. That I was her "model patient." She said this was because I did everything she said, and that I really WANTED to be better. Not just for my sake, but for the sake of my husband, my children, and our ministry.

During those terrible years (roughly a decade), I learned so much. I learned that no matter the havoc that a sin stained world brought into my life with sickness, that GOD IS GOOD, and that I CAN TRUST HIM. I learned that in my deep suffering, I could serve God. That serving God was not about what I could DO FOR HIM, but rather the relationship of my heart to His, during any and all circumstances. **I could praise Him just as well, in my dark sickroom, unable to move, as I could, singing all the songs, writing all the books, and serving all the people that a life of opportunities might produce.**

So many people came alongside of us to help. I learned to receive that help, hopefully with grace and thankfulness. People did my laundry, my shopping, my cooking, my cleaning, took my children to the park, to the library, to church, to museums, and to their lessons. Other people helped home-school my children, brought me meals in bed, took me to the doctor and patiently loved me, when there seemed to be nothing else they could do. To attempt to name the names of all these dear people would be folly. They know who they are and I have thanked God for them thousands of times.   What a blessed woman I am, to have had each one in my life.

It was a gradual recovery, and here, more than 22 years later, I still have waves of nausea, fatigue and muscle pain that come over me, like a tidal wave on the beach, engulfing every part of me.   But I am SO much better.   I have learned to trust God and to know that He knows what is best for me.   I have learned through this weakness, that my God is very great, and that I can trust Him.   I have also learned the lesson of how to be INTENTIONAL in all that I do.   When you only have a minuscule amount of energy every day, you learn that you must "spend it" wisely. I learned that if we were going to have a sweet family time together, at the end of every day, I would not be able to use any energy talking to a friend on the phone, or accepting a visitor in the afternoon.   I had to be very intentional about choosing my priorities. I have learned well, I hope, how to manage myself, and my life, so that it can be the happiest life possible for me, as well as the most useful to others.

This has been my lifelong lesson, and why I am writing this book.   I hope that others can learn from my pain and struggle, so that they themselves will not have to go through the agonizing journey of personally learning this lesson.   There are no promises in this life, except God's promises. When life gets hard, the Lord will be our Teacher if we stay close to Him.

We all love to be happy, to laugh, and to make delightful memories that we can treasure. But when we suffer, that is when we grow as people. God has given me a peace in my heart that is more valuable than all the happy circumstances put together. A faith that is unshakeable. I have learned to trust God in the dark places.

Other health issues, compound these viral and autoimmune system troubles. I have since been diagnosed with Irritable Bowel Syndrome, a hiatus hernia, a heart murmur and a serious nickel allergy. I am to avoid stress, because it affects my life and my quality of life very seriously. Anyone else married, with four children, and told to avoid stress? Good luck with that!

Apparently, Elisabeth Eliot made this her daily prayer, "Lord, have mercy on me". She knew that without the mercy of God, things would go much worse for her. The truth from God's Word, is that I can expect kindness from NO ONE except God Himself. And we all know that I don't deserve it from Him! When other people are kind, we thank God, but we cannot expect it. Life is hard. Life is not fair. One day, our Creator and Judge, will make all things right. My Bible tells me so and so I believe it.

I'm writing this part in case any of my readers struggle with M.E. or other autoimmune diseases. Our mind is where the battle is fought. That does not mean that our illness is in our mind. It DOES mean that our mind can somewhat control the capabilities of our body. I struggled with this years ago. In my diary I wrote,

"Why can I not stand up in church to sing with the congregation, but yet I can manage to play a game of badminton on a Monday night?"

It has a lot to do with messages not getting to the part of my brain that processes information. In a church service there was noise, light, and activity overload. If the messages were not getting to the part of my brain that can think about more than one thing at a time, the part of my brain that can be creative, or the part that handles bright lights and loud sounds, then I would crumble under the circumstances. I learned about putting mind over mood. Notice here that MOOD does not mean depression. I learned, that when I was overwhelmed by my environment, I would not feel depressed. I would have a rush of anxiety and adrenaline that absolutely exhausted and overwhelmed me, making me incapable of doing anything else. I learned to eat because it was the right thing to do. And sometimes eating would take up every ounce of energy I had. A five-minute conversation would leave me limp and drained. There were days when I had to be carried up and down the stairs by my husband. Occasionally my five-year-old would have to undress her worn out mummy and then put her to bed.

The last time I saw the Special Diseases doctor, eight years ago, he told me that I had improved but that he could tell I am not yet better, because my hands stay so very cold. Stress brings on the skin tingles, the headaches, the foggy brain and the muscle pains. The Special Disease doctor told me a story about the Generals who came back from the wars. These men coped brilliantly under pressure, and they executed their job to the letter, and yet six months after they returned, they would literally fall apart. Now in the 21st century we may understand this as post-traumatic stress disorder, but the symptoms are very similar to the symptoms of ME. My doctor compared me to these people, highly resilient and able to rise to any occasion. Again, I am writing this in hopes of someone else reading it and finding help and comfort. There is so little in the medical profession for those of us who suffer like this. I want people to know that there is hope for at least some recovery, and that adjusting to a new normal is okay.

The last time I water skied was in 2006. I got up on the skis, went around in one circle behind the boat, desperately hanging on. But I did it. My family wrapped me in a beach towel afterwards, I cried for a long time from sheer exhaustion, even though I had loved being able to do it, and then crawled into bed and slept for hours. Our expectations of ourselves may need some adjusting, but if there's something I really want to do, I go for it!

Online I once read about the *"Spoon Theory."* I wake up every morning, and may have only 12 spoons to spend that day. At one point, just getting dressed would have used 7 of them. I would have had 5 left to spend very wisely throughout the rest of the day. If I had a three-minute ski behind the boat, that probably used all of my spoons, as well as borrowing some additional spoons from tomorrow's allotment. I learned to be intentional about how I spent every one. (*Spoon Theory* created by Christine Miserandino for her website, www.butyoudontlooksick.com)

Don't be afraid of suffering. Just ask the Lord to prepare you for it, so that when it comes (because it will) you'll be ready to trust Him in it. I would go through every day of this again, because through it all, He taught me that He is good and that I can trust Him.

In Job 23, amidst Job's horrific suffering, he said,

"I look forward, but He is not there. Backwards, but I cannot perceive Him. I cannot see Him on the left or the right. But He knows the way that I take, and when He has tried me, I shall come forth as gold!"

(Job 23:8-10 - paraphrase mine)

I'm know that my God is there, even when I can't see Him. He has never left me alone.

Not once.

Chapter, the Tenth.

Rest in God alone.

Surely I have composed and quieted my soul; Like a
weaned child rests against his mother, My soul is like
a weaned child within me.
(Psalm 131:2 - NASB)

There are a lot of well-meaning people out there.
People who have an uncle who has the same
symptoms as me, or a niece, who takes "such-and-
such" a supplement, who is now completely well. I
have been told that I was depressed; I have been
told that I would just get better if I confessed my
sin, and I have been told that if I had enough faith, I
would be made well. After more than 22 years, I
have learned to smile, thank the well-wisher, and

just get on with my life. If the best doctors in the United Kingdom can't fix me, who are STUDYING Chronic Fatigue, I am no longer putting my "hope" in every quick fix that every other person suggests to me.   Please don't take offense at that, if you are one of those well-wishers.   We had a Special Disease doctor who told us once, "If it is dangerous to your health, or costs a lot of money, don't do it." I have already spent TOO much money, and had my hopes raised TOO many times, to take quick fix remedies seriously.   If all the doctors that I have seen can't "fix" me, and if God chooses NOT to heal me, I realized I needed to stop grasping at straws. I am ill. I am managing.   If God wanted me to be well, I would be well.   My God is so good to me. I choose to trust Him, and Him alone.

And the reality?   The reality is that this body does not define me. One day, I will have a new body, in which no sickness dwells. Praise God.

I want to rest in God alone. I choose to not live my life striving for what is not mine and for what has not been given to me. I choose to live my life learning to observe God, obey Him, and to be very careful not to forget Him. This journey has taught me that it's not about what I can do for Christ, but rather, it's about who I am IN Christ. God is kind, because it is against His nature to be anything else!

So I must draw near to Him, and draw from Him, for the strength to live my life serving others. He has shown me, over the years, that as I do this, He will meet every need that I have.

Resting in God alone, means that I am not going to live my life wondering why I never got my "big break." I don't want to waste any time wishing for things that were never meant to be. What a waste that would be! I want to take what God has put right in front of me, and do that WELL. The God Who loves me, made me, and has placed me in a certain location in the world, into a certain family, with certain gifts, abilities and resources. My job is to look around, right where I am, and get stuck in! Let me give an example here. Many people have the musical skills to be as good or better than anyone who you might hear singing or playing on the radio. But a door of opportunity has not been opened to them. They have not met the right people, or been in the right place at the right time, for that opportunity to happen. I would rephrase that and say that God has simply not opened that door for them.

If this sounds like you, relax. It's okay. God has a plan. It says in Matthew 11:28 to take that yoke off! Stop worrying and obsessing about these things! I can trust God. That is not a cop out, or a lazy option. In 1998 I learned a valuable lesson from my one-year-old little girl, Heather. She used to hate being put into her crib with a pile of books and toys for what we called "room time." We wanted her to learn to amuse herself, and not have to be entertained by others all the time. One day it happened. She stopped throwing all of her toys and books overboard and just screaming. She started to play happily with her toys and books. There was some great play going on. She finally learned to focus on what was right in front of her. That's what I want to be like. To look at what God is doing, and what He places right in front of me. I want to get busy with that, being resourceful and creative to make something good, out of what I have been given! Thanks for the lesson, Heather.

Why have I spent so much of my life caring what people think of me? Let's call people like this, people-pleasers. Or, what about the people that are always needing the approval of others, to feel like they are doing well? Finally, after we had been in ministry for 20 years, I understood that I was free from religion, and that it was simply about walking with Christ. Religion never gets us anywhere, except to show us that we will never measure up. My husband says that religion is simply man's attempt to please God. There are always rules to follow and the next hurdle to cross before a person feels like they have "done well". The problem is, that as soon as a person gets across the one hurdle, then there is another to jump over. It never ends. Why do we get so caught up in the expectations of others, or feeling like we need to please God or please people? I believe it's just because we want others to approve of us. But as soon as we jump three feet high, someone comes along who wants us to jump three feet and two inches. It never ends. I choose to rest in what Christ has done for me on the cross. I recognize that nothing I do can satisfy the expectations of others. I will choose to rest in God alone. I'm not good. Sure, I sometimes do good things, but I will never be perfect. I choose to rest in Christ alone.

Heather, the aforementioned daughter, has had several surgeries in her lifetime. On one such occasion, her scheduled surgery at Great Ormond Street Hospital for Sick Children was the same day as the day of the great bombing at the Russell Square Tube Station in London that killed 56 people. In God's great wisdom, and His plan for us, the hospital rescheduled the day of our surgery to exactly two weeks before that day. We should have been coming up out of that tube, underground station, at the very time of the bombings.

Don't ever let someone tell you that you should not go somewhere because it is not safe. Nowhere is safe. And anywhere is safe if you are in God's loving Hands. Step into the adventure that God has for you. You are SAFE IN HIS CARE!

Have you ever seen a baby that was not yet weaned from his mother's milk in his mother's arms? He will not rest until he finds that milk. He cries, he searches, and he will not settle until he is satisfied. Contrast that with the child that has been weaned. He rests quietly and contentedly with his mother, and he wants nothing else than to nestle against her. He is relaxed, at peace and needs nothing more.

While you have been reading this, things may have entered your mind, that you know you need to give to God. Are there areas of your life which you are holding back from Him, because you are not sure you are ready for Him to have His way there? Perhaps you have a child wanting to go far away to college. Perhaps one of your children wants to be a missionary in other land. It could be that God is asking you to do something, and you think, "Anything but that, God." Whatever God is asking of you, write it down here. Face it boldly.

Ask Him to help you trust Him with this area of your life right now.

_____

_____

_____

_____

_____

_____

Anywhere is safe if you are in God's loving Hands.
Step into the adventure that God has for you.
You are SAFE IN HIS CARE!

Chapter, the Eleventh.

My weakness.   His Strength.

"This is what the Sovereign LORD, the Holy One of Israel, says: "In repentance and rest is your salvation, in quietness and trust is your strength."
(Isaiah 30:15 - NIV)

Have you ever just been overwhelmed by the goodness of God in your life?   You are blessed. You are loved.   You are overwhelmed.

I have seen the Hand of God at work in my life, since I was a child.   I knew what it felt like to be in His will, and to experience His pleasure. God gave me the abilities I have, and I was learning to use them for His glory. In the movie, *Chariots of Fire*, Eric Liddell said,

"Jenny, you've got to understand. I believe that God
made me for a purpose. For China. But He also
made me fast, and when I run, I feel His pleasure. To
give it up would be to hold Him in contempt. You
were right – it's not just fun.
To win is to honour Him."

And I've learned that when I do what God created me to do, I also feel His pleasure.

The turning point of my life was when I was laid low with ME. At that point, everything I was doing to serve the Lord stopped. I had no strength to continue with the worship ministry, the visiting of the elderly, the caring for the young mums and their children, the organizing of the church services, taking sick people their shopping, or anything else that was considered a good, useful act of service. I had nothing left to give, and people were serving me. I had to re-examine what serving God really looked like. In 2 Corinthians 12:9, Jesus said to the apostle Paul, "My grace is sufficient for you, for My power is made perfect in weakness." (NIV) I had no strength. All I had was weakness. The world hates weakness. It would have us be strong and confident in our own abilities. My experience with Jesus teaches me something contrary to this. Jesus teaches me that when I am at my weakest, He shows up and is strong and I am seriously humbled by His goodness in my life.

I think back to an evening rally in India. We were performing on a stage in the open air. Hundreds of people were there. Our generators stopped working and we had no power. We were talking and singing and preaching and praying, but didn't even know if they could hear us properly. We chose to trust God and carry on with the program. This was an amazing night, filled with people coming to faith in Christ. God worked powerfully. We were weak, but He showed up, strong and mighty, and we knew that all the glory was His. The salvation of many souls that night had nothing to do with the strength and beauty of our performances. It was all of Him, and Him alone.

After I became so ill, I remember many days, just getting out of my bed, and crawling into my baby Elizabeth's room. I could not walk, nor could I lift her out of her crib to hold her, but I wanted to be near her. I remember sitting by her bed, touching her through the bars, and just looking at her. I was often too exhausted to even speak to her, but I wanted to be there for her, more than anything.

Once a few years later, when I was able to go to the grocery store sometimes, as the main event of my day, I remember wilting in the middle of my shopping. I sat down on the floor in the shop, not caring what anyone thought, because I did not have the strength to carry on shopping, not to mention pushing my cart to the check out, bagging my groceries, or driving home.

When Heather was born, I remember the duty nurse coming into my room and telling me off for not picking up and holding my baby. Heather was in her hospital crib, connected to feeding tubes, because of her cleft palate. I had just been through a rather traumatic labour and delivery, and the nurse simply had no concept of the fight that was taking place within me, to trust God with this difficult situation and my own utter helplessness.

Oh yes, I've learned that my God is strong enough to carry me through anything. My weakness shows His Strength and I've learned to GLORY in HIM. I am no longer afraid of my weakness, because I have learned that when I am weak, God is there. I want to say with Paul, "Therefore I boast all the more gladly about my weaknesses, so that Christ's power may rest on me." (2 Corinthians 12:9 - paraphrase mine) It's not about what I can do for Christ, but rather – who I am in Him.

When my Dad went home to be with the Lord, I marvelled at the strength God gave me, to pay tribute to Dad, and to play and sing at his funeral service. When exactly three weeks later, to the day, I was playing and singing at my husband's dad's funeral, I was in amazement at how the Lord was carrying me. My weakness truly is an opportunity for God's mighty power to be seen. I have no doubt that He was the One who carried me through every minute of that difficult time.

"But as for me, the nearness of God is my good; I have made the Lord God my refuge, that I may tell of all Your works." *(Psalm 73:28 – KJV)*

One evening, my mother and I were having a sweet time of devotion together. I read Psalm 121 aloud to her. It says,

---

"I lift up my eyes to the mountains—

where does my help come from?
²My help comes from the LORD,
   the Maker of heaven and earth.

³He will not let your foot slip—
he who watches over you will not slumber;
   ⁴indeed, he who watches over Israel
   will neither slumber nor sleep.

⁵The LORD watches over you—
the LORD is your shade at your right hand;
   ⁶the sun will not harm you by day,
      nor the moon by night.

⁷The LORD will keep you from all harm—
   he will watch over your life;

the LORD will watch over your coming and going
   both now and forevermore." *(Psalm 121 - NIV)*

When we had finished reading the passage, she
said, "Well, that's pretty clear."   I remember saying,
"Yes, all we have to do is lift up our eyes to Him, and
He promises to do the rest."   It was sweet.

Oh the fickleness of my own changing heart!   I
seem to understand that He is strong, and that I
need to glory in His strength.   Then somehow,
before I know it, I am trying to be the strong one all

over again. When I glory in my own strength, somehow God seems to slip into the background where He will often stay, until I notice that He seems far away. At this point, I repent of my self-reliance, and come back to Him in humility. Seriously – He's God and I'm not, and who do I think I am anyway, to be taking charge? I'll only mess it up, without His wisdom and Presence to guide me. Here's a real prayer that I recorded in my personal diary one day not too long ago.

"Yes, Lord, I've been overcome by a moment of despair twice today. I choose to STOP, and say, Lord, please take over. Fill my mind with truth instead of despair filled lies. Lord, You ARE Truth. You are the Author of truth. Teach me how to listen to You."

I am blessed if my strength is in God. Anyone whose strength is in God can pass through the valley of weeping. The place of sorrow and pain will eventually turn into a green, lush valley of beauty. There is so much suffering in this world. But God does not waste anything. His Word shows an amazing picture of suffering being turned into something beautiful when our trust is in God.

Suffering is NOT a dry place. Growth happens there!

My conclusion here is to say that suffering is a good thing when it leads me to Christ. I throw myself on His mercy and find peace in His Presence. I'm okay with being weak. It's a place of intimacy with my Saviour, Jesus Christ. If I had never suffered, and noticed my own weakness, I may never have run into His waiting arms.

Chapter, the Twelfth.

Have a Passion for the Lord.

(My personal devotion to Him.)

*"I'm sitting with a coffee and the BOOK that feeds
my soul – praying for the blessing of the Lord to
make us whole."*
(Waiting on Him - VHG)

Years ago, when Heather was a baby, she developed a bedtime ritual. When she was ready to sleep she would bunch all of her cotton blanket up in a ball, lay on top of it, and then use her arms and legs to pull all of the blanket corners in, so that she could cuddle ALL of the blanket at the same time! She wanted it all. And that's how I feel about life. I want all that God has for me. I don't want to miss a thing! I have asked myself when the best time to love God would be. You hear so many people say that they're going to get right with God after they have all their fun, and live their life, doing things their way. Well, I believe that the best time to love God is right now. Today. I want to be so single-heartedly devoted to Christ, that I won't miss a thing that He has for me! The Bible teaches that the blessing of the Lord makes us rich!

God is so much bigger than any man-made tools that we could devise, or any religion we could create to try to get close to Him. If we try to put God in a box, then we ourselves become the losers. We cannot wrap our feeble, earth-bound minds around the greatness of God. The only way I am going to be SURE that I am not creating a god for myself, and imagining what I want god to be like, is to be a woman of the Book, meaning, of course, a woman who reads her Bible every day. Many people prefer to create a god that is convenient for themselves. They may say, "Oh, God won't mind it if I just live like this," or, "if I just follow this list of rules, then I'm sure God will be happy with me." No, no, no. The only way we can get to know God, is through the written revelation of Himself in the Word of God, the Bible.

Our dear family friend, and adopted Indian mother, Tara Theyagaraj used to say, "No Bible, No Breakfast!" In other words, make sure that you prioritize your day with the Living God as the Front and Centre of everything that you do, by reading His Word first thing every morning. From about the age of 11, she read the entire Bible through, once every year that she dwelt on this earth. She's in Heaven now, with the Lord, and doesn't need to read it anymore because she lives in His Presence! I'm not a stickler for what time of day I read it, so long as I have it in my schedule and make sure that it happens! My thinking gets cloudy real fast when I don't structure it around the Words of God.

I recently read 2 Chronicles 38. Did you know that in the generations before Josiah became King, the Word of God got LOST in the House of God? We wonder how that could possibly be, but it happened. When the Word of God was found, the boy-king Josiah commanded that it be read to the people. Oh, how I pray that that God's Words will never get lost in my house! What a tragedy. Several years ago we were challenged by a dear friend to do a speedy Bible read through. For us that meant to read the entire Bible in three months. It was absolutely a game changer for me. My friend Liesl and I committed to this quick Bible read-through. Once a week we would meet for 30 minutes. We would simply share an overview of what God had taught us. That experience showed me the power of the Word of God in a way that I had not seen before. I started thinking God's thoughts. No joke. I was so full of His Word, that it was in my thoughts, my dreams, and coming out of my mouth. It was amazing.

Martin Luther said something like this - If you want to hear God speak, read the Word of God. If you want to hear God speak audibly, then read the Word of God out loud. (summary mine) It's powerful. Powerful enough to change my life. I am living proof of what God can do in a life.

Besides just doing a read through, there is another Bible study method that is so simple that a child can do it. Pick any passage of Scripture. Read it and then ask yourself the following questions:

- **Who?** (Who is this written to and who is this talking about?)
- **What?** (What's happening here?)
- **When?** (When did this happen?)
- **Where?** (Where does this take place?)
- **Why?** (Why was this happening?)
- **How?** (How can I apply this to my life?)

If you answer these simple questions, God will meet with you, and you will never be the same. Guaranteed.　When I was about 16, I remember my girlfriend Liz and I meeting together to use this exact method of study.　We studied the entire book of Hebrews and it was unforgettable.　Well, an encounter with God always is.　Unforgettable.

Another thing I always do before I read the Word of God, is to simply pray and ask Him to open the eyes of my heart to His truth and what He wants me to see.　The Spirit of God will always lead me to the Word of God.　If I'm seeking my answers anywhere else, then the answers I'm getting are probably not the best that God has for me.　And if I read it without asking His Holy Spirit to illumine me to the truth in it, I may miss something that He had for me. I don't want to ever do that.　And just one more thing I want to say about this.　I may regret things in my life, but I will never regret one minute spent in God's Word. It is life and breath to me.　His Word is my very sustenance.

Here's a very clear example of personal devotion.

February 5, 2009 – "It was like this. It had been a long day. After 10 hours out of the house I arrived home exhausted. I lay on the floor, too tired to think, unaware of anything. After a while I realized that my sweet Golden Retriever, Shelley, was standing over me, intent watching, ready for any words of instruction that might issue forth from me.

"Help" crossed my mind, but to be honest, I was enjoying her presence near me too much to even say that. And then I realized a beautiful truth. I was her master. She was ALWAYS watching me. No matter what room I was in, she would position herself so she could see my face, so she could be ready to do my bidding. Her eyes rested on my face. Does it give the Lord that same amount of pleasure when my eyes are resting on Him alone, waiting for the next word from Him? I want to position myself so that I can see the Lord all throughout this day. I want to know His voice so well, that I can hear a whisper from Him at any moment.

Thanks for the lesson, Shelley."

I remember Beth Moore telling a story once about herself and her children. They wrapped themselves around her legs. She was walking around her house. She was doing all the work. All they had to do was hang on. What a great picture of us hanging on to our God. We've been given the easy part!

Ever feel lonely for Jesus?

This is my prayer for everyone reading this simple story of mine,

"Lord, give us hearts for You. May our souls be bent towards heaven today. Fill us up with Your Presence so that we need never be lonely again. Please give us souls that are bent towards YOU!"

Write your own prayer of devotion to God below.

_____

_____

_____

_____

_____

_____

Chapter, the Thirteenth.

The Cost.

"And everyone who has left houses or brothers or
sisters or father or mother or wife or children or
fields for my sake will receive a hundred times as
much and will inherit eternal life."
(Matthew 19:29 - paraphrase mine)

Is there a cost to following the Lord?   Yes, and
don't believe anyone who tells you otherwise.
Jesus, Himself, said there would be a cost. Oh yes,
there will be huge blessing too, but I believe that on
earth, leaving brothers and sisters and parents is a
huge cost! Jesus said to count that cost.   He wants
wholehearted devotion, but wants us to be real
about it. That's what I'm doing here. I'm going to
record some of the costs of following His plan for
my life.   I'm not complaining, just taking stock and
keeping it real.

I often prayed that the sacrifices that Wyatt and I have made would not be to the detriment of our children. When my children did not have believing friends their age, no extended family to fuss over them, and when they lived all squashed up in a little house, I would ask the Lord to take care of their hearts. When I felt starved of God's creation – the mountains, the ocean and the woods – Wyatt would remind me that I AM surrounded by God's most precious creation, <u>millions of people</u>, most of whom do not even know who Jesus is.

I was very aware that it was not my children's choice to be raised in a family in full time ministry. I am still very aware that our choices have been costly for them. Our children did not get to know their own extended family because of the distance between us all and the expense of the travel. They all have their own stories to tell about how the Lord used their upbringing to bring them to Himself, and of course their own struggles along the way. God has showered His mercy on each one of them. I'm going to encourage them to tell their stories, but know that they are not mine to tell. That's for another book, that one day they may choose to write.

Bringing up children in a completely secular society, without family support is a huge challenge. They grew up with few Christian friends, if any. They learned to think like the locals, because we certainly spent more time with the people who lived right near us than ever we could spend with the Church. Our children did not learn to value and understand the cultures in which Wyatt and I were raised, or to appreciate what we had grown up loving. When you live in another culture you are always different. No one anywhere seems to think you fit in. That can be hard for teenagers. We have probably all experienced that to one degree or another. For me, not being able to keep in close touch with school and college friends sometimes meant losing those friendships. People move on and life changes things.

There are also challenges with moving a lot. We have not only moved across the road, but to different countries, and that brings so many challenges, including new friends, new church, new home, new doctors, new neighbours, and new routines.

There is an interesting flip side to this. I remember the day I saw it for what it was. Pride.

We had followed the Lord. We had done what He had asked us to do. But I began to feel unappreciated. We had sacrificed much, and had it really made a difference? Did anyone really care? The flame of my pride was fanned. Was this the pride of Job? Job had not turned his back on God, but he sure could list all the good things he had done. He said he had been upright, and that God had blessed him. To recognize this pride and to realize that we had done nothing, but what God had given us the strength to do was humbling and a very healthy reminder. It's not about us. We are simply tools in His hands. And it's such a privilege to be a tool in His hands.

Through the years, I especially wanted to be around women who could teach and mentor me. You know, the "older teaching the younger" scenario. There never was one close woman who took me under her wing. Rather, the Lord, in His wisdom, sent me several women. They popped in and out of my life, when the Lord knew I needed some guidance and help, and I am so grateful to Him for knowing my needs better than even I did. When I was learning to parent toddlers, the Lord sent someone to suggest a great parenting course. When I had teenagers, the Lord brought a godly woman alongside of me to encourage me in that. When I struggled in my marriage, there was another dear friend who talked and prayed with me. And there were so many others.   Women who cared, just like the women who ministered to Jesus when He was on the earth. They came alongside of me with a timely word and hands that offered help. God has made my life so rich through these women. In Jeremiah 3:15, the Lord tells us that if we return to Him, that He will give us shepherds after His Own heart, who will feed us on knowledge and understanding.   This is what I so desperately needed, so far away from my family, and the Lord sent me these women to nurture and teach me. God is a good, good Father.

My parents let us leave to go to another land with their blessing, knowing that we never might live locally again. They prayed for us daily, supported, visited, and encouraged us. They have been our cheerleaders throughout our entire missionary lives. (Not to mention my whole entire life before that – they are pretty awesome!)

We longed to give our children a stable upbringing, that included a familiar home, lifelong friends, and close extended family.   But we gave them something very different. We gave them the world. Their horizons are broader and they have friends across the world and three passports, not including their citizenship in Heaven.

What if, in paying a cost, we gained MORE than we could have ever LOST?

If I can accomplish anything with this book, then I pray that my readers will make up their minds to be resilient.   To never let ANYONE or ANYTHING keep them from doing what God is calling them to do.

I think of Wyatt's & my dear friend, Ron Hills, who just recently went to Heaven. Ron lived most of his adult life paralyzed from the waist down. Before his accident, he had been one of the Queen's guards. He was our friend, we saw him often, and yet I never saw his wheelchair. He was mighty in spirit, and trusted the Lord, so somehow it was easy to see "past" his wheelchair. I taught children's clubs with him in England. He did not let his wheelchair define him, neither did he allow his constant pain to keep him from doing what God had called him to do.

And what about Terry Fox? The resilient Canadian man who battled cancer, and made it his goal to walk across Canada, with one leg, in order to help others who were fighting that same battle. His 143 days across Canada, before his journey was cut short, gave hope to millions of people.

To wrap this up, take a few moments to list the costs in your own life.

Have you given up a great job promotion, to take a lower paying job but to spend more time with your family?

Maybe you have sacrificed to help your extended family with their needs. I know many grandparents today who are raising their grandchildren, for one reason or another.

Maybe you struggle to make enough money, to support your family in another country. You hope that one day they may be able to join you in your current country of residence. We knew many such people in London, England.

Maybe you are taking care of a spouse who is ill, and you really don't have much time for yourself at all.

Maybe you are in a marriage where you feel unappreciated and unloved. But you keep giving.

The options and opportunities for sacrifice are endless. Let's put this in perspective. Jesus Christ paid the ultimate sacrifice when He died on the cross to save us. He rose again from the dead, so that one day, we too might be raised to life that will go on forever. In the light of His great sacrifice for us, everything good we have ever done pales in comparison. Let's follow Jesus' example and give, expecting nothing in return.

Take a few minutes to list any of the costs that you are aware of making in the space below.

_____

_____

_____

_____

_____

Now write down something that you would never have gained if you had not paid a cost.

_____

_____

_____

_____

Chapter the Fourteenth.

24/7. The Struggle.

Being intentional is such a lifelong lesson for me that I'm going to tell you why it is such an important passion of mine.

I have Attention Deficit and Hyperactivity Disorder (ADHD).   Those who know me best do not doubt it. As a child I just looked like a little shy girl who would get caught up in her daydreams. I was able to hyper-focus on things I was really interested in, like my music, and managed to "get by" with everything else.   I would go, go, go and then go some more, until I crashed.   This was a consistent pattern.   My husband was the first one to ever bring it to my attention. Of course, at first I denied it. When I was young, I was very self-conscious of being slow, and to be honest, tired of being teased about it. I could never listen to music or the television while I was studying, and whatever I did, I poured myself into it 100%. Silly things would seemingly just fly out of my mouth and that also made me feel very stupid. I would impulsively jump on a new thought or idea, learn everything I could about it, before moving on to the next topic. Until I had checks and balances in place, I could not save money. There was always something that needed to be purchased because I just had to have it.

People joke about having ADHD, but when you actually have it, it doesn't feel funny at all. Let me describe what it feels like. The thoughts in my head get all tangled up. My mind is always so busy, that it can be overwhelming. Imagine having thoughts and ideas from every year, every place you have ever lived, every room in the house, and every responsibility in your head all at the same time, clambering for attention. This is ADHD. You know that you have SO much to do, but then get stuck (or hyper-focused) on one thing. Then before you know it, your husband gets home from work and you have not yet put the chicken in the oven. I know this is not politically correct, but I'm saying this about myself, okay? Don't judge me, but sometimes I wonder if I'm going crazy. Yes, I have ADHD, but do all the thoughts in my head have to play AT THE SAME TIME? Take all the thoughts that a person has in a day, and imagine that each thought is an iTunes track of its own. The problem is, all the tracks are playing at the same time!

How does a person learn to cope with ADHD? Well, I have learned to be very intentional about everything that I do. I have learned that the only way for me to accomplish anything, is to be determined, focused and very inwardly resilient. I must want something badly and train myself to focus on (or at least keep circling back to) my goal. My own mother always has told me that I do way too much. She quotes the old adage, "If you want to get something done, ask a busy person." Busy people have to organize their days. And it is the same with me. The only way I get so much done, is by training myself to be very organized and intentional. I seldom just let a day pass, without a plan. Let's say that the following thoughts are in my head for today (and by the way – this WAS a real day).

"I need to send out ministry receipts. I must pack to leave Georgia for 2-1/2 weeks on Thursday. Prepare to drive Heather to college in Wisconsin. Make sure I pay all household bills before I leave. I want to make sure that all my students have what they need before I leave the country. Also work out my teaching schedule for next month. Cleaning up Christmas and putting it away must be done. Will I work on my American citizenship this year? Get caught up on the laundry and iron Wyatt's clothes. I sang a duet in church this morning – still thinking about that. Is that grand piano going to be an option for us? Pray for the people I love and want to help so badly. I am learning to be Wyatt's personal assistant for the ministry. Visiting the doctor for current health issues. What does each child need today? Does Wyatt need anything? What should I make for supper?"

And the list goes on and on and on, with every thought fighting for the supremacy over the others.

How do I cope? I am a perpetual list maker, sometimes on paper, on a cork board, a chalkboard, a computer or an iPhone. Whatever works for me that day, is what I do. And because I always enjoy trying new things, it helps me to get more done by changing it up. Often. When I am really needing to be productive I use the "List of Threes" method that I started years ago. Three things are not overwhelming to me. I can pay three bills then cross them off my list. I then may iron three items, then cross 'ironing' off the list. Then I will write three thank- you notes, for example. My list of three things usually takes about 20 minutes to complete, so if it's something like laundry or supper prep, then I just do that for 20 minutes. This method is huge in helping me get to the end of the day, and to know that I have accomplished something!

I really think the key to coping well with ADHD is to have these methods in place, but to keep changing them up, so as to never get bored. (I always told my kids they were far too intelligent to ever be bored, so I guess I'd better take my own advice!) Another key to living well, for those of us with ADHD, is to make sure that we take good care of our souls. If our needs are met and our souls are happy and at peace, we learn not to strive so much. I had a dear friend who was always doing crazy and silly things. My husband said to me, "I've noticed that Ella is always scattered, but looks so poised and together. You're just the opposite," he said, laughingly. "You look so scattered but are really together on the inside!" Best compliment he ever gave me! If your core values are good, and you're living what you say you believe, this will help you live WELL. It's true for everyone, but especially for those with disorders like ADHD. My soul is grounded, so I choose to have more self-control. I know that it is good for me.

A lot of times I forget to eat. I was really tickled by Matthew 16:5, which I discovered recently. Even Jesus' disciples forgot to eat sometimes!

For several years now, I have been setting a new goal for every year that comes. Something that will take one year to accomplish, if I'm going to do it well. One year I learned how to knit socks. Yes, I knit them quite well, but have pretty much given up on knitting anything else. Ask my girls. I'm not too good at sweaters. One year I decided I would learn how to teach music well, after being a musician for my entire life. I created a system and a style and have been at it ever since. This year is the year of the organized house. I am purging our home of things we do not need, and categorizing things that we do need. It's coming along quite well, but I have to work so hard at it!

I'm always looking for things, and even though I am perpetually trying to organize my things, I have necessities all over the house. Sometimes I forget where I put things. I now have a *Tile* in my purse, and one on my keys. My cell phone can find the *Tiles* and the other *Tiles* can find my phone. It's a great invention. Buy one for $25 on Amazon! I remember the day we were looking for Heather's immunization records for college. It could have taken hours, but we found it in the third bag we rummaged through. The Lord knows my frame (and my ADHD) and led me straight to it. I can't tell you how often He helps me like this. It's so important for me to be a woman of prayer who prays about everything!

I've learned that I need to live a balanced life. It's important to get enough sleep, and to not ever eat too much, anything too fatty, or anything too sweet. My brain functions better when I follow these rules.

I am happiest when doing several things at once and AM ALONE. I can only do several things at once when I am alone. For this reason, I love my at-home time, when I can prepare for the time ahead, whether it's teaching, or throwing a party, or preparing for a music concert. I need that alone-time before I can function well in a crowd.

The real truth is that I am okay with having ADHD. I have embraced who God has made me to be, and have learned to find the benefits of a difficult diagnosis. God is my Teacher, and He teaches me every day how to live with intention. Living with this condition has taught me to be determined and inwardly resilient. I guess you could say that I am a prime example of what the Lord can do in someone's life when they fill their mind with His Word, and trust in Him to get thru every day. I love that I have the ability to hyper-focus on something. Right now I'm focusing on getting this book out. I work every day, and when I have an extra 10 minutes, I'm right back here, sitting at my computer. I can focus on something for a very long time. Sometimes my family thinks that the house could crash down around me, and that I would still be giving all my attention to my music. If you have never hyper-focused on anything, then please let me explain. When you hyper-focus, it's like nothing else in the world matters.

Wyatt has often said, that "when Vicki makes up her mind about something, then it WILL happen." What that tells me is that people need to make up their minds about more things, more often. That's being intentional. Focusing on the important things.

Here is my motto. "Live Well. Until Bedtime."

It's that simple.

Verse 17 in Colossians 1 comes to mind.

"He is before all things, and in Him,
all things hold together."   (NIV)

God is supreme.   If He can hold the universe
together, then I KNOW He can hold me together.
He is God. He is amazing.   And I can trust Him.

Lord, please help me to trust You.

What if, in paying a cost,
you gain more than you could have ever lost?

Chapter, the Fifteenth.

Teamwork.

Teamwork in families.

My Wyatt is a really great guy. We are a team.
After being married for more than thirty years, we
know how different we are, but how those
differences are our very strength. Imagine if we
were exactly the same! If that were true, then he
would not be able to be strong when I am weak,
and vice-versa!   We did the Myers-Briggs
Personality test a few years ago. I came out as
100% artist, and he came out as a visionary and
executive.   Now tell me – who but God Himself
would put two so VERY different people together?!
It certainly wouldn't happen on *Christiandating.com!*
So, we're learning to embrace those differences and
to accept one another as we are.

My job is to stand by my man. Not to try to change him. Do I want him always trying to change me? Not on your life! So, I have learned that we are happiest when we embrace our differences and work together. He needs me to help him whenever and however I can. Now, he does not necessarily need all my comments and opinions, (what man does?) but just to be with him, doing life with him.

I want to work hard at being my husband's best friend. When my children go through rocky times in their relationships, and when things come up that could divide them, I want them to have my example of standing with my husband. No matter what.

Funny how, nowadays, strong male leadership is often considered insensitive and controlling to many women. Yes, it's true that we want our men to be sensitive, understanding and caring. However, sometimes when they appear to "take charge" are they not just trying to take care of us, girls? Let's let them!

God created the institution of the family. Families need to be there for each other, when everyone else has gone home. Whether you're standing in a crisis, or at the brink of a challenge, it's your family that needs to be there. Many times when life is hard,

Wyatt will gather us all together to pray. We know we have an enemy and that Christ gives us the victory. He won it for us on the cross. So we get together to share and to pray for one another, and these times are so SWEET. Maybe because we are not always together anymore, and praying together is the best way of bonding that we know. Besides this, we firmly believe that God answers the prayers that we pray together!

It's so very important for us to be intentional about relationship. My brother Brian is really good at this. He has a no-cell-phone rule when he spends time with his grand-kids. Because of this rule, they actually talk, laugh, sing and tell stories while on car rides. Ever gone into a restaurant and seen a whole family – mom, dad, and all the kids – on their cell phones talking to other people who aren't even there? Yup, it happens all the time. Well it's time for us to try doing it Brian's way. Turn off the cell phone and talk to one another. It may seem hard at first, but it'll get easier as you practice it. Ask the right questions and you may be surprised at how much people like to talk about themselves. You will learn so much, and they'll start learning how to ask you questions back! What a concept!

Here is a sweet note, from our daughter Anne, that I have hung on to, because it reminds me of the beauty of family taking care of each other. She says,

> "Please take care of yourself now and rest up. Since you've been pushing yourself and working so hard, make sure to take things extra slow, okay? You know that I will help you do things, and Elizabeth and FW can help out with driving, so please relax with a good phone call to your mother, warm blankets, a purring Jenny, and a good cup of something warm over the next few days. Love you lots, Anne."

Yes! I was exhausted from being extra busy, and she reached out to me, with encouragement and tangible offers of help and support. A family member that says "I love you and I've got your back" is even more meaningful than support from anyone else. Most family relationships have history, memories, and a deep understanding that comes from knowing background real life experiences.

Even though my sweet Daddy is already in heaven, I often ask myself, "What advice would Dad give me about this?" I had 52 wonderful years of him pouring wisdom and practical knowledge and love into my life that I can still draw from. If I ever find myself stressing about something, I often have his voice in my head about what the sensible thing to do would be.   I'm so glad that he and my mother gave me so much good advice over the years!

Teamwork as neighbours and friends.

Good conversation is people sharing ideas together, listening with respect when others talk and learning what you can from them. The most wonderful example I have of this is the time we visited *L'Abri* school in Switzerland.   Francis Schaeffer had already gone to be with the Lord, but his wife Edith was there, and one of their children, I believe.   Edith Schaeffer (she was in her 70s at that time) taught a class that day, and it was the most amazing lecture I have ever attended.   My mind did not wander one time, which is a rare thing indeed. After the class the staff of *L'Abri* and the Schaeffer family invited us to share a meal with them. I have never forgotten the conversation that we enjoyed around that table.   Many of us had never met before that day, but the depth of the conversation and the sharing of ideas was truly a feast.   How I wish that the art of conversation would be rekindled in our day-to-day lives.   How I want a life in which meaningful discussion features every day.   I want people to feel cared about, as I make an effort to show an interest in them for the unique individual that they are!

We have always tried to work on our relationships with our neighbours. In 2007, Elizabeth and Heather took part in a play in a local village hall. We invited some of our friends and neighbours. I spilt tea all over myself during intermission, so I jokingly told Elizabeth's 13-year-old friend, that if I won the door prize, she would have to go up to the front to collect it for me. Imagine my surprise when they actually called my number! She bravely did go up to the front to get it, and of course we shared the basket full of goodies. These are the kinds of things that build bonds between friends and neighbours. Is there a new movie out that I really want to see? Well, instead of going by myself, I try to think who I could take with me, to help me to get to know them better. Do I accidentally discover that my neighbour's hot water has been turned off? I should invite them to shower at my house. Is there an elderly woman on my street who cannot get to the store? I should offer to pick up what she needs the next time I go! There are so many opportunities to build a sense of community in our neighbourhoods, if we just keep our eyes open. I have also noticed that when I pray for my neighbours, I seem to be more aware of what their needs might be as well. It's like I'm more "tuned-in."

When I turned 40, a godly older man named Jim happened to be visiting us at the time. He was 82, and a newlywed, full of energy and passion for life. He told me very emphatically that I was just getting going good! We need to make sure that we have older people in our lives to teach us from their life experience. Many have the godly wisdom which is just what we need to freshen our perspective!

I'm going to be really vulnerable here and tell you my major flaw. I don't really care what people think about me, who I am not that close to. I try to encourage everyone, but if they don't receive the encouragement that I give them, or if they don't like me, I try to just move on and not take it personally. But what about those people who are the closest to me? I fear that I will not be good enough, or DO enough, to please them. I never feel that way about God. I know his love is unconditional. Why should the people closest to me make me so insecure? I confess. I want to be adored and very safe in my closest relationships. Slowly, I am learning, that if my own husband or children or parents cast me out, I need to be absolutely secure in the love of God.   Period. If I can give to those around me, my family, neighbours and friends, without expecting anything in return, my God will fill me up.   The strongest teams give to one another, but in a real life situation, somebody may not choose to "give back."   I need to be okay with that. To trust God that He has my back, even if no one else does.

Teamwork in ministry.

(Living as the Body of Christ.)

Have you ever made a *"Mind Map"* on your iPhone? I recently started making them this year as a creative way to make a list, or to get a project completed. The main idea sits in the middle of the mind map. Other ideas branch out from the centre. If we could only see the mind map of how one life affects another life, we would be astounded.   It would never end, depending on how far you are willing to trace back through the months and years of your life.   We each affect those around us in profound ways, and we may never know how we have influenced or guided someone else.

Teamwork in ministry is essential.   Any man that tries to be a one-man-show is weaker for it.   Take me, for example. I am quite good at a lot of things, but know that I am master of none. I need to come alongside of people who have strengths I don't have in order to produce a better product, come up with the best plan, or to just be able to get something done more quickly.

My husband's strength in ministry is to invite others alongside of himself.   Although he is a gifted speaker, he invites others in to work with him. Because of this, his ministry over the years has not only been very strong, but very INTERESTING. You bring together the Body of Christ, gifted in diverse ways, and the needs of the entire Body will be met. 1 Corinthians 3:5 says that "each of us did the work that God gave us to do." (NLT) Well, in order for everyone in the Body of Christ to do the work that God gives them, the leadership must be open to whatever God is calling His Church to do!   Wyatt understands this, and I have learned so much from him about teamwork in the Church.

It takes a lot of humility for a person who is a leader of leaders to defer to someone else's way. Especially when that person has so much experience and knows that he/she can do it easily and well.   It takes so much grace. We need to make room for others to flourish and grow in our circles of influence. When we do make room for them, we can benefit from their input, and our ministry will have farther reaching effects because we are working together! Seriously, we need to push others out there and watch them shine. We need to recognize our weaknesses and let others be strong when we are weak. It's okay. We don't have to be amazing, and we sure need to avoid the current trend to put ourselves first. Let's remember humility.

I want to make time for relationships. And I want to encourage others in ministry, trusting that God will receive the glory that He so deserves.

Remember: Every unseen task is for the Lord as well as every SEEN task. Your seen tasks may not be appreciated. Your unseen tasks may not be noticed. It doesn't matter. Do them anyway.

Pride is dangerous. It will get in the way of giving God glory EVERY TIME. There are many pastors we have seen, all over the world, who are territorial. They have their patch where they minister, and they don't seem to like to share very much. Seriously? There are enough needy people to go around.

Let's work on our teamwork skills, and accomplish more together than we ever could, alone.

Wyatt & I have been willing, over the years, to open ourselves up to potential problems for the sake of the Gospel. Inviting others in is risky, but well worth the risk. We have to just obey the Lord's leading in our lives, and trust Him with the outcome. We do not always see the whole picture. Betrayal has come when we have invited others in occasionally, but trusting God through those hard times reminds us of how trustworthy He is, and we are left knowing that He is good, and that we only want to trust Him more. Betrayal can leave a person with an inferiority complex and insecurity about exploring any new relationships. But hey, life is hard. Bad things happen. I say that the benefits of teamwork FAR outweigh any pain that might be incurred from a relationship gone sour. The best policy is to put aside the fear of what others may think of us, and to be vulnerable for the sake of others and for the sake of the gospel of Jesus Christ. He is worth any cost I may have to pay.

Emmanuel and Associates has been building and sending teams to Great Britain since its inception in 1984. I call Wyatt the "connection man." He hears of a need, and finds a solution that will meet that need. It may be a church that has not had a pastor for 100 years. It may be a choir that is wanted to sing and reach out to a community in the Welsh valleys. It could be that a door-to-door team is needed to canvas a community with the Gospel of John. Sometimes a team will be sent that can do physical labour and church repairs. We have conducted football camps and Holiday Bible Clubs for children. Nannies have been found for those who have needed the help when they are in the thick of ministry themselves. The scope of need is as deep and complex and varied as people themselves. No two people are the same, and neither will you ever see two church ministries that are identical.

I have been on dozens of teams in my lifetime. I have always been amazed at how God puts them together. The gifts of the Holy Spirit are fully present when you put any one team together in a location at which they will be serving together. In any given team, you will see leadership, faith, service, encouragement, exhortation, and so the list goes on. God is the One Who builds His Church, and the Gates of Hell will not prevail against it. (Matthew 16:18 - paraphrase mine)

Now it's time to make it personal. Write your thoughts and answers in the space provided.

Think about your family today. Is there one thing you could do, to show a family member that you've got their back and that whatever they are going though, you will promise to be there for them?

_____

_____

_____

_____

Thank God for the neighbours and friends He has put into your life. Ask Him if there's anything you can do to give back to them today, or to help make their load a little lighter. _____

_____

_____

_____

Can you think of anyways that you can promote teamwork in the Body of Christ this week? Is there someone that you can nudge forward, to do what God is calling them to do? _____

_____

_____

_____

_____

_____

_____

_____

_____

Chapter, the Sixteenth.

The Road to Recovery.

I want to address the subject of recovery. When the average person talks about recovery in my world, they have probably just had a week-long bout of the flu or maybe at worst, a chest infection. When they talk about recovery, they are looking forward to feeling as well as they did before they got sick two weeks ago. I want to address a different kind of recovery. This is the kind of recovery a person has when it is impossible that their life could ever be similar to what it was before a traumatic event or illness came to overshadow their life, months or even years ago.

First of all, let's call this trauma what it is, and face the facts boldly. There came a day when I realized that my life is SO much bigger than I am and that I can't control everything that happens to me. When

Adam and Eve sinned, sin came into the world, and every person thereafter was born into sin. God gave Adam and Eve choices, and they blew it. We should never blame God for all the suffering we experience. He is so loving that He chose not to make Adam and Eve into robots.

And THIS is what they chose!

Accept the WORST scenario. The worst scenario is that I may never get better. Am I chronically ill? Yes. **Can I live my life like this? Yes.** When the day came that I realized that the road I had been given was hard, and I understood that I could expect nothing from people or circumstance, I was in a good place. It was time to deal with it and move on. Here's what I did. I grieved for what had been lost. I grieved for what I thought would now never be possible. And I asked myself, "What is the cry of my heart in this moment?" For me, it was in this moment that I decided to live well. My body may not have stamina, and it may be wracked with exhaustion and sometimes pain, but do I have choices? You bet I do. I can choose my outlook on my situation. We've all met the strong resilient people who seem to have nothing going for them except that they are a delight to be with. They have a smile on their face and a kind word to share, and are genuinely interested in us as people. I would venture to say that this person is not just naturally like this. They have made a decision on how they are going to face the world and people every single day. Think of the opposite type of person. The person who complains about everything, who always expects the worst and has a sour disposition. I've learned that in order to be positive and the kind of person that people may want to be around, I have a choice to make. I need to fill my mind with the truth of God's Word and choose to be positive and caring. It's not about me. Everyone we meet is dealing with something. Sure, they may not actually be dealing with a cancer diagnosis, or anything so terrible. Maybe someone just cut them off in traffic, but in their mind at this moment, they ARE dealing with something. I want to choose to be kind.

It has been said that after a period of grieving, a person needs a full year, to have a birthday, a Christmas and so on, before they are really ready to move forward. Even after this full year, a person's day to day recovery is going to look very different from one person to the next. I may not get any better than I am today, but we've only got to take one day at a time, right? One foot in front of the other. For me, every morning is the same. I say with the Psalmist in chapter 43,

---

"Why are you in despair, O my soul? And why are you disturbed within me? Hope in God, for I shall again praise Him, The help of my countenance and my God." *(Psalm 43:5, NASB)*

This verse is amazing. The Psalmist is looking within himself and talking to his OWN SOUL. He instructs his own soul to Hope in the Lord! He reminds himself that the Lord is his only Hope and that he can get through this day with his God there to help him. Notice he even says that the Lord is the help of his countenance. That means that when life is hard, the Lord will help him to put a smile on his face. Really. It's possible to feel your worst, and to smile for the sake of others and for the glory of God.

Ok, so after I have this conversation with the Lord, and before I move and put my feet on the floor, I then make a plan for what I'm going to do first. I make a "list of threes" in my head. First I will go to the washroom, then make a cup of coffee, then read my Bible. The list in my head is simple.

Washroom, coffee, Bible. I can remember three words. Washroom, Coffee, Bible. And she's off!

As I'm sitting with my coffee, reading my Bible, I may read something like Matthew 6:31-34.

"Do not worry then, saying, 'What will we eat?' or 'What will we drink?' or 'What will we wear for clothing?' . . . Your heavenly Father knows that you need all these things. But seek first His kingdom and His righteousness, and all these things will be added to you. So do not worry about tomorrow; for tomorrow will care for itself. Each day has enough trouble of its own." *(NASB)*

So I make mental notes for myself from this passage. This is true. I CAN trust God today. Do I have faith in what I cannot see? I realize that as my faith increases, my worries decrease. Every time. I realize that worrying makes me weaker and even SICKER. I choose to let the joy of the Lord be my strength today. (Nehemiah 8:10 - paraphrase mine)

I remember the days when I could not even read. Even listening to someone read was overwhelming. The plethora of words would overwhelm my tired mind. And so I would open my Bible and pick out one word. That's all I could handle. It might be 'love,' or it could have been 'peace,' or simply the wonderful Name of Jesus, but I would hang on to that word for the rest of the day. It was enough. The Lord meets us where we are, whether we be the most intelligent scholar or the simplest child. He understands. And in my illness, He would sometimes just give me the one word, from His Word, to get me through a very long day. When I had a better day, I would listen to someone reading the Bible online. There is always a way to fill your mind with good things, if you are determined enough.

I wanted to really "LIVE," so I found myself doing whatever I was doing really hard. What I mean by that is doing it with all my heart and soul. I would work hard, or play hard, and then just crash. Was there a remedy for this? I'm still working on it, but I try to just do the things that I think are important, and then say that it's okay to let myself crash. I try to plan and make time for margin in my life. I'm back to teaching music lessons now, a few days a week, and I purposefully do not cram them up close to each other to fit as many into my day as possible. Instead, I give myself margin. Time when I can sit in my car and rest, eat, or just do something other than teach.   Margin is the key to helping myself function well and be the best that I can be.

I have M.E. moments every day.   When I get too tired, because I have been talking too much or exerting myself physically, my original symptoms come back from my original virus.   I feel like I have the flu, a chest infection, muscles and bones that ache, a sore throat, headaches, a fuzzy brain, and an overwhelming exhaustion that cannot be explained. My Gramma Hall used to say she had that "all gone feeling."   I now understand what she meant. In spite of this, my memories of precious times serving and giving far outweigh my memories of my ME moments.   I am learning to recognize what puts me "over the top."   It is an accumulation of thoughts, data, life and responsibilities.   If I make a plan every morning for that day, it helps to keep me from getting overwhelmed.

The dog that the Lord sent me in 2006 became my recovery dog. She got me out of the house when I would not have pushed myself to do so otherwise. She needed me and loved me when everyone else in my life seemed to need something FROM me. What a blessing she was. If you are in a dark place right now, I would seriously recommend a recovery dog, a dog that lives only for you.   A dog that will help you push past what you want to do, for your good AND for their good. For example, is a walk good for them? Well, it's good for me too.

When I was still too ill to do much, but was able to walk short distances, my husband Wyatt took me on a three day getaway without the children. We were walking through the town of Rye on the south coast of England one day. In the window of a newsagent was Jean Guichard's photograph – *Phares Dans la Temps - La Jument.* It immediately ministered to my soul. I saw myself as the man standing outside of the lighthouse. There were torrential waves all around him, and it looked like there was no hope of a rescue for him. I knew that my only hope each day was in God alone, and I identified so strongly with this photograph, that Wyatt purchased it for me. It became the symbol of recovery to me. Underneath the photo, on the frame, I placed the Scripture verse from 2 Samuel 24:14. It says,

"Let us now fall into the hand of the Lord for HIS MERCIES ARE GREAT, but do not let me fall into the hand of man." *(NASB)*

Yes! I could die tomorrow or not for another 40 years, but I can trust myself to His keeping. David was saying that he would rather fall by the pestilence then raging in the land, than to fall into the hands of a merciless person. So true. God is always kind and good. People are not always kind and good. "Oh, Lord, keep me safe in Your care" was (and still is) the cry of my heart.

C.S. Lewis wrote, in *The Lion, the Witch, and the Wardrobe,*

> "Safe?" said Mr. Beaver; "Don't you hear what Mrs. Beaver tells you? Who said anything about safe? 'Course he isn't safe. But he's good. He's the King, I tell you."

This is the perfect picture of my God. The only one who can protect me from the greatness and awesomeness of God is God Himself. That is why I so wholeheartedly throw myself into His care.

Knowing that I might never be able to return to my "before M.E. state" I realized that I needed to think about the things that I CAN do to help myself. Well, I can exercise to keep my muscles strong. I can eat healthy foods. I can sleep. Oh, how I love to sleep. Wyatt says he is going to make a sequel movie to *Sleepless in Seattle* and call it "Sleeping in Atlanta." But it's okay. I have finally understood that it's okay. I also try to avoid all allergens that are known to me, and I can treat any symptoms that I have. Doing these five things helps me to feel more control. I can take charge of how I feel, and take care of myself, even if I will never completely be free of my chronic illness. Being proactive is good.

You know how, when you're on an airplane, they do the safety demonstration? They tell you to make sure you put your own oxygen mask on, before helping the person beside you. Well, at first I was so sick, that I had to concentrate on learning to take care of myself. Once I did that, then I was able to care for my family. There was a time when intimate conversations with anyone outside of our family absolutely exhausted me. So I learned to keep walls around myself so I could function. People would ask if they could pop in for a ten-minute visit and I would say "no," because I was beginning to understand that my family had to come first. Now when people say that they really are too sick to see me, I believe them. Priorities are essential when you're just trying to make it through another day.

At this point, I want to include a caveat about counsellors. I am the first to say that counsellors are wonderful and have helped me tremendously. But for all those people who run around from conference to conference, and counsellor to counsellor, hoping to find the answer, may I remind us all to just run to Jesus. Learn to say, "For THIS (whatever circumstance) I have Jesus." Counsellors have helped me in my recovery, and have taught me how to think correctly about things. But the bottom line is this – Jesus has to be the starting place. He is the middle and the end. Trying to achieve wholeness without Him in our lives is like trying to fix a leaky boat by taking water out of the bottom of a holey boat with a teaspoon. It is not going to happen. When we look backwards, to our own life history, we should only do it to trace the path of God's goodness and His grace in our lives. What's the point of bringing up old wrongs except to forgive them and move on? In 1 Corinthians 14:3-4, Paul says that he does not even examine himself. He lets the Lord do that! So healthy counselling would be to teach people about how GOD views them, and not to spend so much time focusing on me, me, me. Let's get into the Word of God, so we can see how God views us. I'm living proof that this works.

Another part of recovery may be learning to do physical things again. People who have had strokes have had to learn to speak again. Those who have the misfortune of an amputation have to learn to use a new limb and maybe learn to walk again. I had to learn to drive a standard manual shift car again. When I was too ill to walk, I was also too weak to turn the steering wheel in a manual car. Learning how to do this and thinking that I probably couldn't do it, was very scary for me. The first time I drove to the grocery store, I had a car full of children. I stalled on the big hill in the town of Chepstow, and a very nice man offered to get into the driver's seat and pull the car to the side of the road. He could have kidnapped my children, but I believe he was an angel that the Lord sent to help me that day. Right then, I wished myself hundreds of miles away and was not feeling too good about learning how to drive again. Fast forward to two weeks later, when I had my freedom back, and was driving myself wherever I wanted to go, I was so proud of myself for not giving up. Recovery requires a certain amount of bravery.

Our minds and wills are so powerful. Sometimes we just have to "make up our minds". When we have done this, the hardest part of a task is already accomplished. One day in 1998, Wyatt and I took our children to Kensington Gardens. It is a quaint old fashioned park, where the Peter Pan statue and the swings that J.M. Barrie donated to the park reside. On that particular day, our son, F.W., banged his head on the see-saw and busted a huge hole into the middle of his forehead. We bundled all the four children back into the car and went straight to Chelsea and Westminster Hospital in London. While the plastic surgeon was sewing up his forehead (the same surgeon who had fixed Elizabeth's ears, a few weeks before) F.W. kept his eyes on my face. His eyes were full of tears, but he did not so much as utter a whimper. I praised him later, and told him that we had been praying for him. He said that he was able to be brave because he "made up his mind to it." The mind is a powerful thing.

In *The Tale of Two Cities*, by Charles Dickens, Lucy is distressed because she thinks her husband is going to be thrown back into the terrible prison in Paris. Her father sternly tells her to command herself. He declares that she is in a disordered state and that she is allowing nothing-at-all to startle her! More than two hundred years later, can we not still command ourselves to get through a difficult situation? We are stronger than we think, and supernaturally strong, when we allow the Lord to be our Strength and Shield from whatever may come our way.

My daughter Anne wrote me a letter in the midst of what was a very dark time for me. This is what she so kindly wrote.

"Despite your chronic illness – you never have let that stop you. You always persevere no matter what. You keep going even though all the obstacles that have been thrown at you. You're SO incredible – don't ever, ever forget that. You put on such a brave face even when you're feeling your worst. You, my dear, are amazing."

This kind of encouragement is why I have such a passion to reach out to others with encouragement. The Bible says in 2 Corinthians 1:4 that He comforts us in all our troubles, so that we can comfort those in any trouble with the comfort we ourselves receive from God. *(NIV)* If God uses someone to comfort my weary soul, do I need to pass on that encouragement? Absolutely!

There was a time in my recovery when I was actually meeting with a recovery specialist. She asked me what I loved to do and I told her that I loved to sing.

She told me that I needed to sing then - She made it sound so easy.   I had not sung for at least four years, because singing is quite emotional for me and takes a lot of inner strength. I went to Zhenya, a young man in our church at the time, and asked him if he would be willing to help me make a music CD. I told him that it had been years since I had played or sung, and asked him to help me.   He said he would love to. Our journey began. Zhenya's favourite word at the time was "interesting" and believe me, that's what our journey was. Remember that this was 1998, and we had a limited budget, and a Victorian church building to work in. We would record one part, like simply a piano backing track, then we would begin to layer the voices on top of each other recording. I sang all the parts, and arranged the songs the way I wanted, and he would sometimes add a bass guitar to it. Sometimes I sang away down in the bowels of the old church building, where all the mice and spiders lived.   Not my dream recording studio. Occasionally, someone in the flats (apartments) above the church would flush a toilet, and we would groan and say, "Just a minute, wait until the water stops running," and then would begin to record all over again. Some days we would work for several hours and have nothing to show for it, but I was doing what I loved and most importantly, I was DOING IT!   It was such a great accomplishment and victory for me to complete that album. Some people have listened to it and told me it was boring, but I didn't care. We had limited resources and it was huge for me.   It was mostly my music, done my way, and it was a peek into my heart and showcased the goodness of my God. Glory to God!

When I finally arrived at the point when I did not need full-time nannies to help me get through a day, I began to settle into a "new kind of normal." That's what Carol Kent called it, in her book *When I Lay My Isaac Down,*   (a true story and a must-read, by the way).   I believe it is right, that a woman's glory is seen when she serves others. She is absolutely beautiful when she serves others, and very gradually I worked back into being able to serve my family full time. We were home-educating all four of our children, and it wasn't easy, but I did what I could and learned to let the rest go. No, I didn't take them to every home-school event, and often other parents would step up to help me. There were several years in there that I was not as tidy or as organized as I would have liked to have been, but I did my best, and tried not to beat myself up about the rest. My children learned compassion by what we lived and I believe that they are better people because of the challenges we faced. They learned to be giving, generous and kind, and I'm thankful for that.

My God is the best recycler ever. Think about it. He never wastes anything. And He can turn the ugliness of our lives into something beautiful and useful. He re-makes and re-uses what we thought could never be salvaged. Praise His Name.

Let's talk about making steps toward any kind of recovery. Prayerfully read the statements and questions below. Write down what God shows you in this moment.

You grieve for what has been lost. Only you can fill in this blank. What have you lost? A loved one, your health, your financial security or _____

_____

_____

_____

_____

You grieve for what may never be. This could be your dreams that can now never become a reality. You may never get to climb that mountain, or grow old with that spouse. Go ahead and grieve for what may now never be. It's a step towards a healthy new beginning. _____

_____

_____

_____

_____

Ask yourself, "What is the cry of my heart, in this moment?"   Can I dare to dream new dreams?

_____

_____

_____

_____

_____

_____

What lesson have you learned in your life through suffering, that you don't want to be wasted?   Ask God not to waste that lesson, but rather to use your suffering to bring about good in your life, and in the lives of those around you.

_____

_____

_____

_____

_____

_____

Learn to say, "**For THIS** (whatever circumstance) **I have Jesus**." Counsellors have helped me in my recovery, and have taught me how to think correctly about things.   But the bottom line is this –
Jesus has to be the starting place.
He is also the middle and the end.

Chapter, the Seventeenth.

Walking in Faith.

Learning how to really LIVE.

"Without faith it is impossible to please God."

(Hebrews 11:6 – NIV)

From the age of 20, my prayer had always been to be gentle and dependable.   Then at the age of 43, I wrote in my diary that my prayer had changed direction. I realized then that I needed to be consistent and full of faith. Well, now, at this present age, I realize that my goal is simply to be full of the Holy Spirit and walking in step with Him. Then all those other bases are covered, right?

I have learned that the only times I feel really, really alive, are the times that I am walking in faith. When should we believe God? Let me rephrase that: Is there ever a time when we don't need to believe God? Christ promises us abundant life on this earth, but it is only ours when we live by faith. I make this simple for myself by saying that I only need to follow God's leading. He is responsible for the outcome! The pressure is off of me. I simply have to trust and obey. Literally.

I have often prayed that the Lord will not let me get by, by trusting in myself. I have also prayed for my children, that none of them will get by, by trusting in themselves, their own cleverness, or their own creativity. And I would pray the same for anyone I loved. The reality of the situation is that living by faith is the only satisfying way to live. When Christ is the object of our faith, our faith will always inspire others. Someone recently commented to me on a website called *Happify*. They said,

"Vicki, you are such an inspiration to me. I love the faith you have and the very natural and practical ways it is woven through your life."

Thank you, *Happify* friend. But, isn't this exactly how we're supposed to be for others? When we experience the love and power of Christ in our own lives, then others will be inspired.

Every step in my life has been a major step of faith. Having the faith to leave home to go to northern Alberta for college was huge for me. Later, believing that God was leading me to India to work as part of a music and drama team was another step. Then having the faith to leave Canada, knowing that my life would never be the same again, was another leap. Then when the board of directors of Emmanuel & Associates asked me what I thought we should do, even though we had not fully raised all of our support yet to live in England, the answer was easy. Full of faith that only could come from God, I said, "I believe it's time for us to go to England." People talk about the great faith that someone has, but let's flip that around for a minute. **If the person knows his God, and that his God is trustworthy, then why should it not be easy to step out where He leads?** He's God and I'm not. I can totally trust His Hand.

I remember when it was the summer of 2000. Wyatt and I and our four children were sleeping in a tent in a little town called Honiton, in Devon. We were awakened by a terrific thunder and lightning storm.

We sang *Who's in the Middle of the Dark* at 2:30 a.m. and then walked across pitch black fields to the toilets in our wellies and under an umbrella. I have put myself in my children's shoes many times, and thought how much they must have trusted me, to make that trek across a muddy field, singing *Who's in the Middle of the Storm*. Well, of course we know the answer. God is.

I remember another time that Wyatt and I took the children out of the inner city of London to go camping for a week. We pulled up in a field, as you do in England, and found the perfect place to pitch our tent. We got all of our gear out of the van and started setting up the tent. It was some time before we realized that all four of our children were still playing in the van! We wondered what we had done to them that they would feel more comfortable on the inside of the little van, that to choose to run and play in the lovely green fields. They were so used to be confined in small spaces and content to play with whatever was in front of them at the moment. They trusted us completely. Faith looks like that.

When Elizabeth was a little baby, and before I had the strength to walk very far, one of my dear friends, Pat, suggested that she would put Elizabeth in the push-chair, and I could try to hang on to the stroller to see if I could walk to the end of the road and back. My little baby had hardly ever been out of the house, and certainly had never been in a position where she could not see my face for a long period of time. She literally screamed all the way to the corner and back. It reminded me that I need to be that dependent on the Lord, that when I can't see His Face, I really want to change positions so that I can!

Once I had to make a trip to the local bakery. I had asked the Lord to use me somehow, somewhere, that day. I remember that the lady in front of me in the queue wanted to talk, and we had an incredibly meaningful conversation. I learned that God will use me if I make myself available.

I don't know what tomorrow will bring, but I know that I don't want to waste today. When we pray the prayers that God wants us to pray, then we know that He will answer! On one particular occasion, we were looking for a used van on the internet, and when I saw the white 1999 Ford Galaxy Ghia, I said, "That's Our Van!" Because I knew it was. I ended up naming it Old Peaceful and it was a reminder to walk in His steps. When the Lord provided my

English Austen Maxi, it was before I knew how to drive a standard shift. The Lord provided an automatic car for me, when automatic cars were almost unheard of in the country of England. When we went looking for a home in Wales, tears sprang to my eyes when I walked into the 200-year-old farmhouse that was Crossways Farm. There's nothing special about me, but I know that when I trust the Lord completely, He loves to take care of me.

Galatians 5:1 says that "it is for freedom that Christ has set us free." *(NIV)*

It's done. If I am in Christ, I can be FREE! I don't have to live under a yoke of bondage to my fears, my passions or to anyone else for that matter. I have been set free to follow the Lord and to love people deeply from the heart, with the love that only He can give. I am rejoicing today in this incredible freedom! Today matters. Loving people and choosing not to be mediocre is an exciting way to live. It will stretch me beyond where I am comfortable, and I will have to trust God. And that's a good thing.

I love our summer mission teams, because they are packed with purpose and many of the distractions of life are removed. Team members don't have to think about what they are going to do each day, what they are going to make for supper, or any other decisions for that matter. There is a schedule planned for the team, and their job is to stay close to the Lord, watching for opportunities to minister to people, as their day unfolds before them. Maybe team life is part of what has taught me so much about living by faith. The big decisions are not my responsibility when I'm a team member and I can just trust God and let Him work out the details. Living life as a responsible adult in the western world usually means that we are constantly making decisions and have so many things going on at once that sometimes we just get ridiculously busy doing nothing of any great importance. Maybe it would be good for us, to ask God to interrupt us, when our "Go-Button" gets stuck, and we have stopped listening for His voice in the day-to-day. What could be better than hearing His still, small, voice in the middle of my day-to-day?

Mamas need to pray. I remember when my sweet F.W. was born. My mother was in British Columbia and I was in London, England. We were EIGHT hours apart, as far as the time zones go, and yet the Lord woke up my wonderful mother, from a deep sleep, to pray for this daughter of hers. I was in labour and delivery at the time. Explain it away, if you like, but I believe that my God loves me enough to wake up my mother, who loves me enough to pray for me in the night watches. Randy Travis sings an amazing song called, *When Mama Prays*. I heard it on a *Touched By An Angel* T.V. episode back in the 90s. It made such an impression on me that I have never forgotten it. (I'm still looking for this song – if anyone finds it, let me know, okay?)

Most people seem to think that God only wants to hear prayers about the BIG things. In our family, we pray about everything, and love to praise God for His many answers! If I am rushed into a decision, then it is usually wrong. But when I finally know what to do, it's always the right thing, and I have a confidence that goes down to my toes and a faith that rises to the Heavens. Here is one such occasion. It was September 2006. We had just arrived home from a lovely vacation in North America, and I was praying diligently for a dog. I knew I was supposed to have one, so I asked God to lead us to the one perfect dog for us. I prayed for a dog with an obedient, gentle soul. It also needed to

have a pleasant and loving disposition and needed
to love us all. I phoned all of the Golden Retriever
rescues in the United Kingdom, because I knew we
could not afford to pay for a pure-bred puppy.
Every rescue I spoke with told me that the only dogs
most likely available for adoption would be elderly
dogs or naughty puppies. I wanted a middle-aged
dog. I kept praying diligently. I also prayed that
the Lord would not give this to me if it wasn't the
best thing for our entire family. On October 5th, one
month from the start of my search, I received a call
from the Golden Retriever rescue in North Wales.
There was a four-year-old Golden, whose mistress
had died, and whose master could no longer care
for her. I prayed fervently all night, as I had to
phone the lady back in the morning with an answer.
My wise husband said yes, but that it would not be
a good idea for us to go to the dog's home and
take her away from her master when he had also
just recently lost his wife. Pat, the Golden Retriever
advocate, agreed to be an intermediary for us. Isn't
God good? The first night that our Shelley was with
us, Heather slept in the kitchen with her. When I
came down in the morning, Heather was singing
Somewhere Over the Rainbow to her. It remained
Shelley's favourite song always. After we got a

dog, F.W. said, "Now our house is a HOME!" And his eyes were shining.

If anyone is looking for an exciting life, I say just walk by faith! That is the way to feel most alive, and to be most useful, in things that matter, in this life. Faith needs to be an integral part of our life, for without faith, we are not really living as God intended. Faith needs to be a part of what dog you choose, which car you buy, and what house you rent. Really.

Let's bring this a little closer to home for you. Answer the following questions in the space provided.

Do you like to feel really alive? _____

_____

_____

_____

_____

When was the last time you felt really alive? _____

_____

_____

_____

_____

What can you put in place, in your life today, that could be a tangible reminder to live by faith?   You know you want to. _____

_____

_____

_____

_____

_____

Today matters. Loving people and choosing not to
be mediocre is an exciting way to live.   It will
stretch me beyond where I am comfortable, and I
will have to trust God.   And that's a good thing.

Chapter, the Eighteenth.

Learning to say, "Yes, Lord."

"Satisfy us in the morning with your unfailing love,
that we may sing for joy and be glad all our days."
(Psalm 90:14 – NIV)

We've been talking a lot about living by faith. Does that mean I am not a thinking person? Of course not. I pride myself in being a thinker and liking to think things through. Let's look at it this way – Even a good leader, will put himself under a "Leader of Leaders" who has his respect and his loyalty. That's why it's so easy for me to follow the Lord – He totally has earned all of my respect and loyalty. Even if He had not proven Himself to me, time and time again, as the living God, He deserves my worship and my submission, just because of Who He is. He is the Intellect who made us in His Image.

He knows everything about everything and is outside of time. I do not have the audacity to challenge His right to lead me. So, I say, "Yes Lord. You are God and I am not. Show me the way."

The oldest recorded book in the Bible tells us about the life of Job. Whenever I think life is hard, I just have to remember Job, to get my "happy back on." He lost his children, his home, and his health. His wife told him to just curse God and die. Job chose to trust God instead.

When my first baby miscarried, I suffered so deeply. I wanted that child. Other people told me to never mind – that there would be others. Or they would say, wasn't it good that it was quite early on in my pregnancy? Others said that there must have been something wrong with the baby, or it would have developed further. You know what? Not one of those comments helped. I wanted that baby and my heart ached with the loss. It was several months later that the Lord revealed something astonishing to me. I was angry with Him. I was angry that He had not allowed my baby to live. This was a huge turning point in my Christian experience. I looked at Job and saw that he could not see what God was doing either. But Job chose to trust God. I was looking all around me for Him, and could not see Him. I got down on my knees and asked the Lord to forgive me for doubting Him. I decided to say, "Lord, You know what You're doing and I choose to trust You. Yes, Lord." It was the best thing I ever did. I trusted Him with my heart. Anne was born nine months later. If I had had my first baby, I would not have Anne in my life to this day. I'm so thankful for Anne - and my first baby? Well, she's in Heaven waiting for me.

One of the most important things to learn is to say YES LORD. I moved away from the most beautiful place in the world to follow the Lord. I can only imagine how stunted my spiritual growth might have been if I had said NO to Him. It's like, when you say YES LORD, that He then gives you more and more experiences and more and more opportunities to say YES LORD. **It's an adventure that you are stepping into.** You don't know where this adventure will take you, but you know it's going to be good.

You could say that we CHOSE to raise our family in England. But was it a choice, really? When you follow the Lord, He just opens the way up before you, and you walk in it. My husband often says that a person should be willing to preach, pray or die at any moment. I learned quickly to say YES LORD, even when I had only been playing the piano for a few months. I was asked to play for children's church. I played, not because I was good at it, but because I was willing. I played piano for a friend's wedding at 19, because I was willing. I sang for weddings because I was willing. I played for funerals because I was willing. On and on it goes. And I believe that the Lord does not measure our talent or our ability, but rather, He is blessed by our willingness. Of course I want to be excellent at my craft. I aim for being the best that I can be. But I always try to remember that it's the attitude of the heart that the Lord sees and loves. Let's just look and see where God is working and ask Him if we can be involved there too! Watch for His Hand, just as He is watching for our willingness!

It's true that the exact way that He made us, is in keeping with how He will use us. DUH! I know He will probably not use me to be a shining light in the building trade. I have no interest, no building knowledge and no experience at all. It makes more sense that because He put a passion in my heart for communicating truth and for music and worship, that maybe He will use me there. But the bottom line is – am I willing to do whatever He asks me to do? Of course the answer should be a resounding, YES.

I want there to be a supernatural quality to my life. I want to live beyond my own capabilities. I want to be reaching for my dreams always. And I want to be surprised by anything that God might do through me. Every project I ever begin must be undertaken praying the whole time, asking the Lord to be in the process and guiding every step of the way. Do I really want my life to be just ordinary? Well, yes, I know I'm human, but I want my life to have the Presence of God in it. To be satisfied with anything else is less than His best.

Having stipulations for my own life is not a good idea. If I'm going to say "YES LORD," that means I need to be willing to do anything, anytime, and to go anywhere that God chooses to send me. Out of this idea, has grown my most quotable quote. Everywhere I go, I pick a home and say, "I could live here!" I want the Lord to know that I will follow wherever He leads. Yes, a nice beach house in Florida would be nice, but hey – I did live in inner-city London for 15 years.

Now let's make this personal. Is there any part of your life that you have been unwilling to say "YES LORD" about?

_____

_____

_____

_____

_____

Ask Him to reveal any of these areas, and to give you the grace to respond to Him about them.

Chapter, the Nineteenth.

Living Creatively.

God is Creator. **He is therefore creative.** We are made in His image, the Bible says. We, however, only have a few short years on this earth, small resources, limited intellect, selective ability, and varied opportunities. Therefore, in order to accomplish anything worthwhile, we must be intentional!

When Wyatt and I were first married, I read a wonderful book by Edith Schaeffer, called *The Hidden Art of Homemaking*. She believed that homemaking was a creative endeavour that involved art. Here is her definition of home making in her own words.

> "I would define 'hidden art' as the art found in the ordinary areas of everyday life. Each person has, I believe, some talent which is unfulfilled in some hidden area of his being – a talent which could be expressed and developed."

In her book there are copious amounts of creative ideas for making the home an interesting and satisfying place to live. I found it absolutely inspiring to realise that I should think about the way I prepare a simple tray to take someone breakfast in bed, or the background music that encourages great conversation. Sometimes it is when the smallest items are carefully thought through that beauty is created and life is richer because of it.

One blessing that came out of my very long illness is that I learned to appreciate the hard work of taking care of a family and a husband. A woman at home is often interior designer, teacher, chef, pastor, accountant and chauffeur, just to name a few things. I educated my children at home, we were in full time ministry, and so on. A woman's job is demanding. It requires brains, strength and discipline to do really well. I will never again apologize for staying at home. I now applaud everyone who makes this their profession and their hobby.

There are endless ways to be creative. When we think of art, we often think of music and painting, but there is such a wider scope for creativity. Inventors are creative. People who make up new recipes are creative. Clothes designers are also creative. Does the list ever end? And if I look at an arrangement of flowers, or read a beautiful poem, these things are also expressions of someone's soul, and are considered art. Here is a list of things that I do in my life, that I consider an art form. You may add your own ideas below, and I would love to hear them! Cooking, sewing, writing stories, writing music, arranging music, writing monologues or plays, writing puppet scripts, leading a choir, vocal performance, card giving, gift giving, making food to share, quilt designing, setting a table properly, greeting someone properly at the door, sending someone back off into the world with God's blessing, background music, floral arranging, good kitchen smells, and proper warm lighting. I consider every one of these things to be an art form, if they are done with intention and mindfulness.

One way to live creatively is to be resourceful. Do you need to make more money to save for next summer's vacation? Think about what you might do to make a little extra money along the way. In the past I have cleaned out the attic and sold things on eBay, Etsy and Amazon. You might also dream up ways to spend less money. When I had four little children at home, we would have sleepovers in the living room, reading *Anne of Green Gables* by candlelight. We would have surprise dinner cafés and watch movies from our air mattresses on the floor. There are so many great ways to make AND to save money. Your imagination is the limit!

I truly believe that everything we do should be an art form. Why should we do anything thoughtlessly? Dig into history and learn from it. Our own families give us excellent opportunities to learn from history and to get great ideas of how we might live our lives in a more creative and interesting way. Make homemade ice-cream. Send an old-fashioned card via snail mail. Re-use items that can be reused - Will they not be more meaningful the second time around? Wrap presents in familiar fabric that will be recognized by the recipient. Leave love notes around for your family. Romans 12 talks about outdoing another in love and good deeds. I want to get creative in my loving, and be that person who looks for ways to honour others.

I do not ever want to let FEAR keep me from being creative, or from doing ANYTHING, for that matter. One of my favourite Jane Austen quotes, from *Pride and Prejudice,* is this.

"We are each of an unsocial, taciturn disposition,
unwilling to speak, unless we expect to say
something that will amaze the whole room, and be
handed down to posterity
with all the éclat of a proverb."

We seem to think, you see, that whatever we create must amaze everyone who hears or sees it. Sometimes we need to be creative, because it is in our nature to be creative, and it is an expression of our souls. It does not have to be for anyone else's benefit at all. We have a very dear friend, Navin, who once told me that it did not matter if anyone else appreciated the music I was writing. He said that my music was the expression of my soul to God, and it was okay if no one else liked it. This was very freeing to me. There is something very vulnerable about creating something – anything – and sharing it with another human being. We instinctively want them to love what we love.

Of course, there is a time when we should share the good gifts that God has given to us. My creativity is not just for me and sharing what I sew, or what I write, or my songs, or my food could possibly be a great blessing to someone else. But when I share what God has given me, I know I should not do it looking for their approval. It's really not about that at all. If I can share a gift or a talent that I have, then let me do it for the benefit of the one who receives it. It may come from my hand, but it's not about me.

Art cultivates more art. In our family we consume large quantities of words. We are readers. We sometimes enjoy looking at art. We broaden our music appreciation by listening to all manner of music. We love drama that is well acted and monologues that are spoken with passion. I have heard it said, and believe it to be true, that creativity always begets MORE creativity. Exposing myself to the creativity of others will inspire me. If I'm going to be creative in my relationships, in my homemaking and in my own ability to create a new song or a new story, I must make margin in my life for creativity. A life that is busy all day, runs to the grocery store on the way home, slaps together a quick meal, spends the evening doing laundry and paying bills before it finally falls into bed at night, may not have the time or the energy to be living creatively. Margin must be a priority in the life of a creative person.

Spontaneity is also essential. Sometimes you have to get out of the routine to remember how to laugh. Really laugh. That spur of the moment trip to the Dairy Queen to get a soft ice-cream cone.   Piling everyone in the car to see the last showing of the movie you've been wanting to see. Going to the beach just so you can feel the wind in your hair. You know the old saying, "All work and no play, makes Jack a dull boy." It's so true. Get creative with your time. You'll be happier, and boy, it feels good to laugh.

I talked to my mother tonight. She said, "I have to go and put my feet uppier." "Pardon," says I. "Yes, uppier," said she, "I made up a new word. Do you like it?" We laughed until we cried. It felt good. She inspired me, so then I tried to make up a word. Oodles was the word. It means lots and lots. You can say it to anyone you care about. I love you lots and lots. OODLES! I've since found out that this word was included in the Webster's dictionary, circa 1800. Well, at least I'm using a word that is "new to me!"

Looking back in my diaries I found the record of an Easter Service that I had planned. It was titled "Love to Live," and I was encouraged to know that being intentional has shown up consistently in my life over the years and that being creative has always been a passion of mine. Sometimes living can be bitter and sweet at the same time. I'm learning to step over the cliff (of faith) and into JOY.

Definitely it is a constant choice to seek God and to choose joy. I want to do both. In the bitter life situations, as well as the sweet, there are true life lessons. I have wanted to creatively teach my children history by sharing true life stories that apply to what they are going through.

For example, I want to share the stories of when so-and-so made a bad business deal by getting financially over-extended, or when so-and-so did not guard their passions and look where it got him. There are stories of how a family got by with very little because they stood by each other in the hard times. Homemade history lessons hit home a lot harder than the history lessons in the school textbook. Because we've met Uncle Bert or Auntie Alice, the lesson will be remembered. That's sharing knowledge creatively so that our children might become wise! Creativity is a way of life.

Living creatively brings happiness to my own soul and to the lives of others around me. Ask yourself how you can choose to be creative today, and I promise you, your life will be a richer place to live because you did!

Let's bring this closer to home now. Make a list of things that you do in your life that you could consider an art form. _____

_____

_____

_____

_____

_____

You can also list any **new** creative ideas that you may want to implement soon. _____

_____

_____

_____

_____

_____

What can you do TODAY to make your life a richer place to live? _____

_____

_____

_____

_____

_____

_____

_____

_____

_____

_____

_____

In chapter nineteen, I shared with you many of my ideas to live creatively. I would love to hear yours! If you would like to share them with me, you can email me at betterthanhappy61@aol.com

I'm hoping that you'll write me! Just put _Unwavering_ in the subject title and I'll be sure to get back to you as soon as possible!

Chapter, the Twentieth.

The Unique Language of a Missionary.

I believe that a missionary is given the unique ability to communicate with people who are in a different culture than he was raised in. It's like understanding a people group that he was never TAUGHT to understand.   This person can see quickly where another individual is "coming from" and somehow use their communication skills to connect effectively. It's like speaking another language that he was never taught.   The only foundation I have, with which to prove this, is my own experience. Human connection can happen even when culture, economic standing and language seemingly should be a huge barrier. Compassion, kindness and love will cut through any barrier, but it will only ever happen when we are willing that it should. Prejudice or fear will always create a barrier and prevent genuine connection from happening.

Having a broad experience of life and becoming comfortable with all kinds of people is something that can be learned if a person is willing. Realizing that it is healthy to expand our own little world is the first step. Yes, there are many people in this world who have lived their entire life within a fifty-mile radius of home, and prefer to hang out with those few people that they know and like. How much richer is a person's life, however, when they look for opportunities to expand their horizons and stimulate their thinking?

I was raised in a wonderful family. We enjoyed a comfortable home, had a holiday at the lake every summer, and I never remember wanting anything that I did not have. We ate meals together, talked about things, and went for long Sunday car rides. My childhood seems euphoric to me now. Call us a *Leave it to Beaver* family. I remember being invited to a girl friend's birthday party sleep-over once. It was my first opportunity to see how other people live. It was a rental accommodation, shabby and not very clean. There were mattresses on the floor. I remember wanting to be this girl's friend because the other children teased her a lot. Her hair was always dirty and she didn't have nice clothes. She was being raised by a single mom and I'll never forget that this mom took us to the local pizza parlour and paid for us all to have a sumptuous feast of whatever pizza we wanted. I can imagine now that their family may have done without many things that month, so that her young daughter could have a nice birthday party. It was my first introduction to the idea that many others were not as fortunate as I.   Soon after that, there was another opportunity for me to see how a classmate lived. She asked me to come home with her one day after school because she said she would be home alone and wanted some company. This girl's home had no furniture and I remember the bare light bulb coming out of the hole in the ceiling. I was shocked that people in my comfortable world could live like this. After that I would stop in at my house after school to get saltine crackers to share with my friend. I don't know what happened to her, but I wish I had known how to do more. Jesus said that the poor would always be among us, but what I learned from these two experiences, was that I wanted to rub shoulders with these people.   I wanted to be comfortable being their friend.

I think about my Auntie Ruth's picture perfect home. I loved visiting her so much. Her family made me feel so welcome. The sumptuous bed and gorgeous food were lovely, but their kindness to me was what really touched my heart. I learned by spending time with different people, on all social levels of society, that it was important to be able to adjust my thinking, to be able to be comfortable in situations where there was plenty, and in situations where there was want. I believe that if we are going to be useful tools in the Lord's Hands, then we need to care about people, no matter who they are, where they have been, or what their values and aspirations are.

People are made in the image of God, and we need to be comfortable with all people, so that we can speak into their lives, if we are given the opportunity. I believe I am just as comfortable in a home in an Indian village, as I am in a Manor House in the Cotswold's. I would hope that I could go into any situation and fit in. At a fancy dinner of upper middle class people, or in the most down home country meeting you ever saw. With a group of musicians, or a group of intellectuals. Let me sleep in a tent, or let me sleep in the grandest room in the Savoy Hotel in London. If we are comfortable wherever God places us, then we can concentrate on the people we meet and THEIR needs, instead of just thinking about ourselves. If my passion is to encourage others, then I will follow their lead, and be more aware of making THEM comfortable with me, than I am about my own comfort.

Back in 387 AD, Ambrose (the Bishop of Milan) told Augustine, "When in Rome, do as the Romans do." Basically, it meant that when you find yourself in a new situation, follow the customs of those who already "know the ropes." When visiting a foreign land, follow the customs of those who live there. This is not to say that I will be like a chameleon who is constantly changing to fit in. I know who I am as a person, I know who I am in Christ, so the essentials of who I am will not alter. My personal values will not shift. It DOES mean that my outward behaviour and conversation will relate well to the people I am with, and not be offensive to the culture as a whole.

In *Pride and Prejudice*, Elizabeth talks about Mr. Darcy to Mr. Wickham. She says pointedly, "In essentials, I believe, he is very much what he ever was." My desire is to remain the same in "essentials" wherever I am, and with whomever I am talking with. I'd like to suggest that the outward way in which a person communicates with others, can change and fluctuate when needed, without the inward character of the person altering at all. Know the truth and stand by it. If you don't know what to say, just speak the truth in love. The truth will do the work. And love always wins.

So how can we best communicate effectively? Be authentic. Real. Communicate to others in a voice that they can understand. Work on listening to others and respecting what they have to say. This hits me the hardest, closest to home. You already know that I have ADHD. I constantly have to work on really listening to my husband and my children. I try to stop whatever I am doing, and listen with my body language as well as my mind. I try to put down what I am doing, turn in my chair, and look at them while they are talking. I have learned that when I am intentional about listening, then they feel more valued and respected.

We have already talked a lot about making margin in our lives for creativity. Sometimes I think it is healthy to study what someone else loves in order to show interest. If a person loves to cook, then ask them about their new favourite recipes. Maybe you know someone who is delighting in a new hobby – ask them how that's going. There is so much that we can learn from others every day, if we just look for opportunities to ask the right questions. Right now, I'm exploring how to put my music on iTunes, so I'm going to find people that know about that. There are so many excellent opportunities to make meaningful human connections with people if we are paying attention!

And I hope I am learning to make every interaction meaningful. I want to keep it personal. One way to do that is to match my enthusiasm to the expression on their faces – this applies to children or anyone! Have you ever had something amazing happen to you, only to share that experience, and have it fall flat, because the person really doesn't seem to care about your latest life changing, transforming, WOW moment?

I spent a long time in 2006 trying to think of how I could bless my dad when I saw him that summer. Finally, I thought of it. He had a favourite happy song that he loved. Mother and he would dance to it, and it became known as "their song." Well, I purchased it on iTunes, and when the time was right, I played it for him. He was not too well at the time, but he recognized *Tie a Yellow Ribbon* and as he listened, his eyes were sparkling. I had found a way to touch his heart and bring him joy! It's all about finding the most effective way to communicate to whomever we are with!

Some may think that this is an unusual topic to address in such a book as this, but I disagree. A missionary is someone who is called to take the gospel of Jesus Christ to those who have never heard. Those people may live on the other side of the world, or they may just live across the street. How we connect to other people personally is huge, in whether they will want to get to know us and come to enjoy a trust relationship with us. Life happens in the day to day, moment to moment encounters. Let's work on being the kind of people that others will want to get to know.

It's time for personal reflection again.

Can you think of any ways that you could stretch yourself to become more comfortable in new situations? _____

_____

_____

Examine your people skills honestly.   What could
you do to improve your skills? _____

_____

_____

_____

The next time you talk to someone, make a point to
make it about THEM. Record your experience here.

_____

_____

_____

_____

_____

Chapter, the Twenty-first.

Broken Together.

"Maybe you and I were never meant to be
complete? Could we just be broken together? If
you can bring your shattered dreams and I'll bring
mine, could healing still be spoken and save us? The
only way we'll last forever is broken together."
Broken Together; Casting Crowns lyric

This pretty much says it all. It describes us all.
Maybe not today, but some day. We have been
born into sin. There will be times in all of our lives
when we have broken minds, broken bodies, or

broken spirits. I'm not being negative, just realistic. Life is hard. We need to help each other through the tough times. We were not meant to struggle on alone.

Sometimes our marriages feel broken. Seriously, is a person EVER ready for marriage? No, but you get married and you learn how to be married. And sometimes in the learning, we get it wrong. It seems to me, that the underlying thread of unhappiness in marriage is often because we want the approval of our spouse, and if we don't get it, it's possible to give up. In other words, we are kind and try really hard with everyone else EXCEPT our spouse. Remember that it's always too soon to give up! When Wyatt and I have struggled the most in our marriage, this was when a break through or serious happiness was right around the corner! Don't give up! And when you get it wrong, remember to kiss and make up. That's the fun part.

What about when our children are broken? Is a person ever really ready to have children? There are so many books and classes and podcasts on parenting, but nobody but me ever had the children that I have. I was learning how to parent these particular children that God gave to me as I went. And I've made a lot of mistakes along the way. I've asked my children to forgive me too, now that they're older, and can understand that I was learning too! I was very aware that every sin and fault of mine seemed to be magnified in my children. My prayer was always,

"Lord, I AM THE PERSON in this house
that I need you to work on,"

because I was the grown up and I knew I needed help if I was going to raise happy, well-adjusted adults! We always strived to make happy memories for our children, and worked really hard at spending lots of time together talking, making things, going on walks, having regular family devotions, going to plays, the library, museums, ballets and the cinema. Our favourite walk was along the River Thames. But you know what I learned? That no matter how perfect you try to make your family, and no matter how wonderful your time together is, you will still experience times of brokenness.

Heather came into the world with a cleft palate, and six weeks later produced a pyloric stenosis, which is basically a super-sized muscle that kept food from entering her little stomach. Her little body was broken and I had to work really hard as a mum to get her fixed. They told me that she just had the flu, but I knew it was something much more serious.

Always trust a mother to know her own baby!   I remember when Anne was 10 years old and she told me that she didn't want to tell me all her dreams because she would fall apart inside. A mum can love and give and support with all her strength and still sometimes not be able to give her children everything that they need. I remember another time that F.W. and I had had a disagreement about something. Elizabeth said, with great philosophy, "If only Adam hadn't sinned!" It took the edge out of the moment and we were peaceful once more. Humour is one of a family's greatest virtues!   Keep it alive!   Once I asked Heather if she had made that mess on the floor and she replied, "Nope, I didn't see me do it!" You have to laugh, and you have to keep loving.   That's what makes it so good.

What about when our parents start to seem broken? Some of us have had the wonderful experience of believing that our parents were perfect - that they never argued in their marriages and that they always knew how to take care of their children. We thought our parents were never afraid and always knew what to do. I wrote this note to my mother once. It said,

"Dear Mom, I'm so glad I can tell you about my day.
Remember when I used to knock on your door at 11
or 12, to come and sit on your bed, and you NEVER
said you were too tired to listen.
What a great Mom I have."

See! She was amazing! But what about now, when she's 89 and her poor body is tired and she can't see her Bible to read it, and I think she must get so discouraged to not be able to walk! She's broken and I need to be there for her. What did we learn when Dad had Alzheimer's? I made bran muffins with chocolate chips in them, for Mom and Dad, and Dad asked mom who that nice girl was that was in the kitchen baking? He didn't always know who I was, BUT I KNEW WHO HE WAS. And it was time for me to give back to him. These were the parents who changed my diapers, kept me safe, taught me to ride a bicycle and then drive a car, and sent me off to college with tears in their eyes. Yes. When we realize that our parents are broken too, it's time to give back! I remember walking into the Evergreen Baptist Care Home, after my dad had only been there five days. His eyes lit up when I came in and he was so happy. I remember visiting Mom and Dad together. We cuddled up and I remember Dad saying over and over, "Pray for Vicki, pray for

Vicki." It was such a tender moment, having him know me and love me like that.

What can we learn when we are broken? We can learn that being enveloped in the love of God is the best place to be. He has forgiven me. He knows all my flaws and failings and can take me, in my brokenness, and envelope me in His arms. There is no sweeter place. When I am broken I yearn for God. I know that He's the only One Who can really fix things and make them right. Here's a prayer that I recorded in my diary, when I knew that we were broken and needed God's help.

"Broken again. Sobbing into my pillow so no one can hear me except You, oh God, my King. I dissolve my pillow with tears. Oh God, you are the only One who sees and understands my pain. Please comfort me, so that I might reach out to comfort others with the same comfort with which You comfort me. Your Word says that You put the lonely in families. Sometimes I think that our family is the LONELIEST place to be. Help me to guide others to You and to recognize when others are lonely too. THIS IS NOT about me and my pain. This is genuinely a cry to You, Lord, desiring that You would shower this broken family with YOUR very great mercy, so that somehow You will receive glory through our lives. Please use every one of us. Be glorified. This is about YOU."

I was yearning for truth, yearning to have God's perspective on the situation at hand. I realize now that family can only be a lonely place when we try to hide ourselves from one another and are saying that we are not yet ready to deal with something. We are getting so much better at talking about hard things. It takes practice. Don't be afraid of those hard conversations. There is a better and a happier place beyond them.

How can we fix what is broken? Well, first of all, I am going to resolve TODAY to be the best wife I can be. The best mother. The best daughter. The best friend. Am I going to mess up? Yes, of course, but the intention of my heart is to be these things and I choose to be intentional about each role that God has given me. I want to always speak the truth and never be satisfied with partial truth (or LIES). In November 1998 I remember waging war with the weevils in my house. I scrubbed, I vacuumed, and I sprayed poison. Still I had to remove all the food from the house. Every last crumb. It was impossible to know what was contaminated and what was not. This was a lesson that I will never forget. We can't always see where the sin in our lives is lurking. We just have to do war on it, because there should be no room for any!

William James, a practical psychologist who lived 1842 – 1910, summed up what I've been trying to think through for years. This is antiquated English, so bear with me, okay? He said,

---

"Action seems to follow feeling, but really action and feeling go together; and by regulating the action, which is under the more direct control of the will, we can indirectly regulate the feeling, which is not. Thus," he explains, "the sovereign voluntary path to cheerfulness, if your cheerfulness be lost, is to sit up cheerfully and to act and speak as if cheerfulness were already there."

There are some people I know who would disagree with this, but I have found it to be true in my own life. Dwelling on the negative helps no one, and choosing to be cheerful helps everyone. I'm not suggesting that we just ignore the hard things and pretend they are not there, but I am saying that using our wills to help us act right, will affect how we feel about things.

Another lesson I have learned is that I need to daily ask God to fill all my empty places. We are all going through something, and I need to stop expecting others to meet my needs! Only God can reach those empty places that no one can see.

And lastly, I want to stress the importance of a kindness filled life.   To look for ways to help others through THEIR days.   Everyone we meet is going through something, and a kind word or kind smile can only make our days better.

It's interaction time again. Consider the following:

Are there broken places anywhere in your family right now? _____

_____

_____

_____

_____

Have you been able to talk freely about these broken places, so that healing can begin? _____

_____

If you have not been able to openly talk, think of a way that you might begin this conversation. _____

_____

_____

_____

_____

Take a moment and ask God to fill up all of your empty places.

He's waiting for you to ask.

Chapter, the Twenty-second.

The Suffering that Leads to a Fruitful Life.

Any suffering that leads us to Christ, and to acknowledge our need of Him, will be useful suffering.

(a tried and true saying by me - VHG)

We all love to laugh. The pursuit of happiness is actually in the American Constitution. We all want happiness. We search for it. Some people go to great lengths trying to acquire and ensure it. We give up some things, in order to increase our enjoyment of life. We tie our priorities into it. We want to be happy and we want to know that we're happy. Talk about suffering and people think that you're really a negative person and a downer. We all want to be happy and to sometimes laugh until our sides ache and tears are running down our cheeks. But, here's the thing. It is when I suffer that I grow as a person. Yes, it's true. We grow as people when life is hard, when we are learning things – when we suffer.

When should I pray? Well, when I suffer, I am driven to pray. That's a good thing. Imagine that I am in the most difficult circumstance that I have ever faced. I feel lost, uncertain, confused and alone. The best place for me to go at such a time as this, is to the One Who knows everything, and can help me find my way through this bog of pain that I am wallowing in.

Have you ever been in a tall corn maze, or a maze of hedgerows in England, such as King Henry VIII devised (so he could play with his wives) outside of his castle? When we suffer, it can feel like we are in the middle of a maze, like we are lost and don't know how to find our way out of it. The Lord God, Who made Heaven and Earth, sees this maze. He knows exactly how to help us, when we are deep within its bowels, and will show us the way out of it.

So, when should I pray?   Always, daily, and moment by moment. I pray as I drive down I5 to Seattle, that the Lord would surround me with His angels and keep me safe.   I pray when my plane takes off, and I ask the Lord to hold my plane up in the air, until it's time for it to come down again! So praying in adversity is not only the answer, but it is a great comfort to my soul.   I am reminded when I pray that I am not walking this difficult road alone.

Humour in suffering is awesome and amazingly helpful. When my mother was so ill in the hospital, after surgery, my brother and I went on a quest for prune juice.   We could not find it in the store anywhere.   Brian suggested that we find someone who looked like they might enjoy drinking it, or might need it themselves. Maybe THEY would know where we could find it! We laughed and laughed, but after the trying and difficult days of being with Mom in the hospital, laughing was just what the doctor ordered.   It was fantastic.   My mother always said, "It's good to laugh. If you didn't laugh, you'd cry."   Find the humour in any given situation and learn to savour the sweetness of even the moments of suffering.

Suffering that leads us to Christ will always be useful. One day a person may be forgotten, but

God IS and always will be. He is ultimately in charge, so, I'm learning to hang on to Him. There is not an individual living who has not suffered, or will not suffer in the future. In this human condition we all we have struggle and pain. There is the pain of chronic illness. Life brings disappointments. At one point, Elizabeth was going through all manner of pain. Although this is HER story to tell, I can only say, that THIS mother was stretched beyond her own capacity to endure. Here is an excerpt from my diary. I wrote this in "real-time" pain.

"Suffering. Inner anguish that no one can see. Pain that goes beyond what words can express. Longing to make some sense out of the dreams that never came true . . . "

"Yes, June has been hard. Maybe these few weeks have felt so strange because I thought I was supposed to be in England with Anne. Maybe because my life, my husband's life, my children's lives are looking different than what I had always thought they would look like. . . SOOOOOO, I've been at home, quietly taking care of little, inconsequential things, and the time has been passing rather slowly. I have filled many hours reading a wonderful book called *Now I Lay Down My Isaac* by Carol Kent. She got a call in the middle of the night saying that her only son, a lovely, responsible, caring young man, had been arrested for first degree murder. It's the true story of her faith walk. She talks about suffering in such a fresh way. She talked about Jacob, in the Old Testament, who stayed up all night to wrestle with God, because he wanted a blessing from God. He limped the rest of his life, but he HAD MET WITH THE LORD AND SEEN HIS GLORY. She said that our limps may be internal, and no one can see them. We ARE limping, but we have seen God's glory. And it is so worth it.

The book of Ecclesiastes, in the Old Testament of the Bible, teaches that without God, life is utterly meaningless. This is why we persevere in our sufferings. Because we want to get past them and because we may have already learned that it is through these hard times that we can draw closer to our God. For those who have never experienced the amazing Presence and love of God, adversity is often the place where they meet Him first. Think about the single mindedness of a mother bringing her child into the world. She knows that soon she will hold her precious child in her arms. The pain is nothing to her, in light of the joy that lays ahead. Christ also said, that He endured the pain of the cross because of the joy set before Him. (Hebrews 12:2) He was thinking about eternal glory! WOW. It's just so rich to be sitting here, filled with the pain of so much difficulty, but knowing that through all of this, we will be drawn close to the Lord. We will learn to rely on His strength and His JOY. . . And it will be worth it all because we will have seen glimpses of His glory along the way."

Here's a favourite song of mine – it is probably familiar to you. It's called *Beautiful Things*, and it was written by Gungor. Let the beauty of the words wash over you, no matter what you might be facing in your life today.

All this pain. I wonder if I'll ever find my way.

I wonder if my life could really change at all.

All this earth, could all that is lost ever be found?

Could a garden come up from this ground at all?

YOU make beautiful things

You make beautiful things out of the dust.

YOU make beautiful things

You make beautiful things out of us.

YOU make me new

YOU are making me new.

My prayer for this moment:

"I want my heart response to be 'Yes, Lord'.

Whatever you have for our family, please teach us.

Don't let us waste any of this pain.

Let every lesson be learned well.

Let every tenderness from Your Hand be delighted in, and given back to You for Your ultimate glory.

Yes, Lord, I choose to worship You."

"When I am afraid, I will trust in You"

(Ps. 56:3 – NKJV)

Chapter, the Twenty-third.

Our citizenship is in Heaven.

"Heaven seems much closer now.

I know some people there" *(Heaven - VHG)*

What is citizenship? When a person has citizenship, it means they belong to a certain nation. If they were out of that country and encountered difficulties, their country of citizenship would come to their aid, if they needed it. There is loyalty of the person to the country AND of the country to that person. I was born a Canadian. If I were to travel to a foreign country and encounter difficulty, the Canadian government would hopefully come to my aid. We are proud of our heritage and where we came from. In the Olympics, for example, a whole nation of Canadians will cheer on a few Canadian athletes. We are interested and stand behind those whom we have an affinity with.

I grew up in White Rock, British Columbia, which was literally on the Pacific Ocean, and two miles from the American border. We would often cross the border and go into the United States. I remember every time we crossed, that the border officials would ask us what our nationality was. It mattered. As a teenager, I remember wanting to tell them, from Philippians 3:20, that my citizenship was in Heaven – which according to God, was the most important country to be a citizen of! It is from Heaven that we eagerly wait for our Saviour, the Lord Jesus Christ, to return for us. If we have put our trust in Him, then He "has our back" even better than the Canadian government would have mine, if I got into trouble. I live everyday with the Hope of going to Heaven one day.

It goes even further than that. The Bible teaches that my citizenship is in Heaven. Right now. Today. Eternal life begins the moment I put my trust in the Lord Jesus Christ. Yes, one day I will go there, but today I am still a citizen. It's like me having Canadian citizenship, but still living in the United States at the moment. It's okay. One day I know I will be going home to Heaven. I have that HOPE.

The Bible teaches that one day every knee will bow, and every tongue will confess that Jesus Christ is Lord. It's so important for us to do that now, so that we are always ready to go to Heaven to be with Him. We never know what a day holds. We think we have 20, 40, or maybe 50 more years to live, but we don't know for sure.

I have lived in and visited many, many places. Sometimes I get tired of not belonging anywhere - of not fitting in. I start complaining about it. I know that Heaven is my home, but sometimes I just want a home here on this earth. So the Lord gave me the desire of my heart. In 2007 we were able to actually purchase our own home. We had rented several homes, or lived in church manses, but He gave us our own home. It was a miracle. But guess what I learned in the process? I have learned that security still does not come from having a place to rest your head. Security does not happen when you acquire a permanent address. My security must still be in God alone. This home could be taken away from us, and I would still be secure.

When our children were very little, every time I was putting them to bed, after we talked about their day, I would explain the Gospel to them, telling them that one day, when they put their trust in Jesus Christ for the forgiveness of their sins, then the Lord would begin to prepare a home for them in Heaven. I explained that one day, when they left this earth, they would have a new home to live in, in Heaven, where there was no sickness, or lying or stealing, and just LOVE. In 1999 Elizabeth succeeded in memorizing John 14 for school. This was the way she quoted the verse - "I go to repair a place for you. And if I go and repair a place for you, I will come again." Well, heaven is one place where no repairs will ever be needed! On another occasion, I was blessing her and telling her a little bit about heaven. As she tweaked the skin on her arm, she asked me if God was going to leave this part of her, laying on the bed when she went to heaven? I said yes, and that the real Elizabeth who lived inside the skin would go to heaven to be with the Lord Jesus. She was so thrilled and at peace about this. Children sometimes can understand the things of God, better than those of us who think we are so grown up and mature!

In 2013, I was headed to a family emergency. My dad had only hours to live and I was not sure that I would be able to get there in time. Somehow, when people find themselves in a crisis like this, they can think more clearly about the things that are really important. I knew that after this day, my life would never be the same again. I recorded my thoughts from that difficult time.

"Looking through the beautiful clouds to the rugged mountains below, I'm thinking how nice it will be, for Dad, and one day for me too, not to be earthbound. With sin engrained in the very flesh that ties us to the world. I am looking down through the clouds, to the rugged terrain below, that depicts tough times, dryness, barrenness and struggle. What a gift to be free of it all and just to be with JESUS. I don't know if I'll get to see my dad again in this life or not, but I choose to trust You. I love you Lord. Thank You that even though Wyatt can't be with me,
I know I am not alone.
Thank you for filling up all of my empty places."

The Lord did something amazing for me that day. As we descended through the clouds, through the misty veil at 30,000 feet, I asked the Lord to show Dad His glory in a way that he had never seen it before. While I was praying this prayer, the Lord took my precious dad into His loving care. We calculated the time of his death later. My sister Wendy was sitting beside him, reading the Bible to him, while I was praying for him. Because he passed away before I landed in Vancouver, I was just overwhelmed by the Lord's kindness, in letting me be a part of my Dad's home-going. Our God is great and so GOOD.

This was the dad that wept every time he told us how the Lord had saved Him. This was the dad that warmly held our hands, when we held his, when it was time to pray. He is waiting in Heaven for me now, and Heaven is more precious to me, because he is there. 2 Corinthians 3 talks about how we reflect God's glory. I would see the glory of God in my father's face when he talked about how the Lord had saved him. He would say, "I was saved, as though by fire." By the "skin of his teeth", is what he meant. I so want to reflect the glory of God. Even just a little glimpse of His glory brightens the face. Remember when Moses went up to the mountain of God, and was given the Ten Commandments? When he came down to speak to the people, he had to cover his face because it was shining so brightly. God's glory can be seen in us when we get a glimpse of Him. Let's remind each other to stay in His Word daily! In Ecclesiastes chapter 8, Solomon reminds us that "wisdom brightens a man's face."   I don't want my face to fade!

It is so true that people who are getting close to dying seem to understand things so much more clearly than the rest of us.   My husband's mother, when her cancer had returned and she knew that she had not very long to live, said passionately, "I have wasted so much time!"   My dear friend, Margot, became very sharp in her mind the very last time that I saw her.   We had this amazing conversation and she gave me very wise advice about our ministry and my marriage, and what I could do to honour the Lord and my husband in these areas.   It was so clearly from the Lord that I was deeply moved and inspired.   She passed away a few days later.

One of the things I have learned to love, is playing piano for funerals. Whether I know the family and the deceased person or not, I love, love, love to be present with family and friends at this tender time. It's such a privilege to learn about how this person made a difference in their world.   It never ceases to challenge me significantly to take up the baton of the person who is no longer present on this earth. For example, if they were a great prayer warrior who prayed for their family, who is going to do that now? Somebody needs to. Maybe it needs to be me. My prayer is that the music that I play or the song that I sing will bring them comfort and point their eyes towards the only One Who can give lasting comfort, and Who will be there when everyone else has gone home, when we lock the doors and turn off the lights at night. Jesus Christ.

My prayer is that the Lord would bend my soul towards Himself and to Heaven. Ask yourself the questions below:

Is your soul bent towards heaven? _____

What could you do today, to make heaven more real to your conscious thoughts? _____

_____

How would being more aware of the reality of heaven, make you able to do more good on this earth? _____

_____

_____

Chapter, the Twenty-fourth.

In the Large and in the Small.

My constant goal is to learn how to savour life. Every aspect of it. Every one of the headings below is typed on a paper and taped to my kitchen cupboards. To me, learning to savour life and all it offers is huge. And learning how to savour the small moments, as well as the large events, requires me to be intentional about it. In this chapter, I want to spend a little time unpacking each simple statement below.

Simple is an Art Form Worth Mastering.

So many people seem to have regrets at the end of their life, because they haven't realized soon enough, what was really important. Well, I'd like to suggest, that it's the little things that are most important. You may have heard the story about the man in the shack, on the beach on some island somewhere. He was offered a fine education, a good job, and beautiful home and a lifetime of opportunities, so that when he retires, he can go a buy some little cottage on the beach and live his remaining days peacefully and the way he wants. I can imagine him saying, "Why would I want to do that? I've already got a cottage on the beach and time to do what I want to do!" Okay, it's a simplistic argument, I grant you, but consider this - why do I have to wait until I'm old before I start deciding to enjoy my life?

For all the people with their big plans and huge ideas of what they want to do in a lifetime – I feel happy for them. But for me – I want to love people, live moment by moment, learn to walk in the Presence of the Lord, and be energetic and enthusiastic about the task in front of me. Doing this, my life will be full and I will be at peace. I definitely think that for some of us, this is an art form that needs to be mastered. If a person is always thinking ahead, or always dwelling in the past, then this will need to be worked on, as any skill is worked on, until proficiency is mastered.

Purge my world.

In this day in which we live, we have so much. Far too much. Have you ever noticed that when you stay in a motel room, or in a vacation rental, how simple life seems? We really do not need 9/10ths of what we have. I have spent years reading about how to keep a tidy house. The one that I get most teased about is called *The House that Cleans Itself*, by Mindy Starns Clark. It was a great book, and I learned from it, but evidently it did not completely solve my problem, or my family would still not be teasing me about it! I highly recommend the book I have just read through twice, if you are in the market for purging your world. It is called *The Life-Changing Magic of Tidying Up* or it is subtitled *The Japanese Art of Decluttering and Organizing* by Marie Kondo. I must say it has been delightfully helpful, and my husband is very happy with the progress I am making! I am very sentimental about the history of my home and the things therein. I want to keep things that make me happy, and that bring back good memories. I have a crystal candy dish that belonged to my mother, for example.

Every time the lid is removed and replaced from it, I get the giggles. My dear Gramma Hall was a diabetic who knew she should not be partaking of much candy, if any. When we were out of the room, and we heard the tinkle of the lid, we knew that Gramma was at it again, having her sugar for the day! Memories like this are precious and if they remind us of our own happy history, then, by all means, let's keep those things! What can I purge from my world? That is what I ask myself every single day. The more stuff we have, the more dusting we have to do. The more items we collect, the more we have that needs to be repaired and taken care of. So I hold something in my hand and ask myself, "Do I REALLY need this?"

Simple is good.

And once you make your life simple – keep it simple!

I actually went through my clothes closet last month. I was amazed at what I could easily give away and still have more than enough. How can I keep things simple? It's about living in the moment. If what I am doing now is important, then I should give it my full attention. I may be washing dishes, writing a song or I may be talking to the next door neighbour's eight-year-old. It matters, and I need to do it well, whatever it is. I love it so much when the power goes out, and we have to live simply. We light candles, play cards, or read a book. Life instantly becomes simple. It's like going back to the *Little House on the Prairie* days. There is no sound of the washer and dryer running, no television and no ice cube maker, making ice. Everything is calm and quiet. You may actually hear the battery-operated clock on the wall ticking, for once! I love going camping and cooking bacon and eggs over the campfire. I love hanging the washing on the clothesline. I love going for long walks. I want to be very intentional about living simply because I am happy when my life is simple. Certainly the American culture praises efficiency. But is doing 20 things at once always the best way? When I slow down, I have time for relationships and for people. My heart rate slows down, and I notice my surroundings, and that I am very happy. Yes, I'm a list maker, but I don't want that to control me. I want to think about what is important right now. I will do that, and be all there whilst I'm doing it.

One thing at a time.

If Billy Graham had the opportunity to speak to
thousands of people in a massive football stadium,
or he was given the opportunity to share Christ with
a single person, in the comfort of his own living
room, which opportunity would YOU say that he
should choose?   Many might say, "Well, obviously,
he should choose the opportunity which will affect
the most people."   I wonder if God views things the
same way that we do.   He knows what the effect
will be of us sharing the Word of God in faith.
Perhaps, in the instance described above, the
person sitting in Billy Graham's living room, might
be the next evangelist, to bring tens of thousands of
people to faith in Jesus Christ.   We don't know what
the effects of our obedience will be.   We do know,
however, that we are called to be obedient.   Truly I
want to make the most of every opportunity, but
God's ways are better than ours. We seize the
moment to do good when we have it, but we should
never look down on (or despise) the "day of small
things". *(Zech. 4:10- NASB)*   Whether I am helping one
person, or a football stadium of people, my attitude
should be the same. If this is worth doing, then this
is worth doing. It's a no brainer.

Let's create a fictional scenario of a pastor of a small church, in a village in England. He faithfully preaches the gospel week after week. He visits the sick and cares for the unlovely. He is worn out, yet he perseveres to share the Word of God with all he comes into contact with, and to practically meet the needs of those he meets. It has been years since he has (knowingly) seen someone come to faith in Christ. The person who he has been taking meals to for years committed suicide. Does that make his work null and void? No, every act of kindness and every word spoken in love matters. Do we dare say that his work is somehow less important, than the work that God has given to the city preacher of a large congregation? Absolutely not! It all matters. We can leave the outcome with God.

Live this moment fully.

I am an artist by nature. I feel the ambiance of a room before I see it with my eyes. I smell everything, feel everything, and live for the experience of it. For me, it's not about getting where I am going, it's about the journey, and enjoying every step I take along the way. Here's a true story. My dog, Shelley woke me up with her barking one morning. It was 3:17 a.m. Assuming

that she needed to go to the bathroom, I bravely
trudged out of bed, put on my winter coat and
Wellingtons (rubber boots), and headed for outside.
It was only after a few moments that I realized the
truth. It was snowing outside. There was a white
layer of the wet stuff on the lawn like a thin cotton
sheet. What I did not know was that Shelley had
somehow sensed it had snowed and simply couldn't
wait another minute to play in it! Wow! I want to
be that eager to live life and enjoy it. The Irish
Minister, Jonathan Swift, author of *Gulliver's Travels*,
once said, "May you live, all the days of your life." I
have thought long and hard about this. My chronic
illness has helped me to process this and make it
real in my life. Every day that I live, I want to really
live. Not exist. Not just waiting for tomorrow.
Wherever I am, I want to be all there. Period.

As a Christian, I desire to live each moment by the
Spirit of God. The Bible says that the Holy Spirit
comes to dwell in everyone who has put their trust
in Christ for their salvation. The Spirit of God will
lead me, and as I abide in Christ, then each minute I
live will become an "abundant" minute. Notice that
several abundant minutes will turn into an abundant
day. Abundant days will turn into one abundant
life! John 10:10 says that Jesus came to give us
abundant life. He wants to give our days meaning.
Let's not sell ourselves short!

One way of living this moment fully is to notice the small things. I notice and enjoy the pattern that the Starbucks barista puts on the top of my coffee. I notice the patterns that the clouds make because Gramma Hall taught me to watch the sky and look for shapes. I remember her seeing elephants one day up there in the fluffy whiteness. She was savouring moments and teaching her small granddaughter to do the same!

I was down on the White Rock beach a few days ago. A musician was playing by the old train station. I could hear the seagulls, feel the wind in my hair, and see the waves crashing in. I sang with the busker and enjoyed the moment fully. We smiled at each other and our souls connected. May we never underestimate the power of a single moment in time.

You know already that I naturally get very distracted. I have probably built the strongest focus muscles ever and have learned to use this disability as a strength. When a person knows how to hyper-focus, they learn to savour whatever it is they are doing. Life's an adventure and whatever I do, I don't want to miss it! I look at my top strengths. They are spirituality, curiosity and a love of beauty. I often ask myself how I can use these traits to live more fully and to be more useful to others. For me, I know that without God, life is meaningless. I ask a lot of questions to learn about my world. And I search for beauty in everything. This is how I live my life to the full.

Living in a state of Gratitude.

There is nothing more intrinsically beautiful than a life of gratitude. To realize that we are not owed anything, and that everything good that comes to us is a gift from God. And we're always thankful for gifts, right? So I want to be grateful for everything that comes my way. Even the bad things that can teach me lessons are something that I can be thankful for.

The following is a prayer of gratitude that I prayed when my beloved dog, Shelley was alive.

"I love Shelley so much. I love the way she smells when I bury my nose in her fur. I love the way she answers back in her throat when I speak to her. I love how her eyes follow me around the room. I love her beautiful face. Thank you Lord for sending her to me, in answer to my prayer. She has taught me so much. Please let

her be my puppy in heaven. Thank you for the
beauty of her life and that I got to be her
mistress whom she loved. Just so thankful."

This prayer was written four months before her death. I thought we were only going to have her for a few more weeks. I'm so glad the Doctor was wrong.

Our minds are powerful tools given to us by God. I cannot always choose the feelings that live inside of me, but I can control my will with my mind. And controlling one's will is huge in living a great life. I've already shared this with you, but in the light of gratitude, I believe it's worth repeating. William James, a practical psychologist summed up what I've been trying to think through for years. He said,

---

"Action seems to follow feeling, but really action and feeling go together; and by regulating the action, which is under the more direct control of the will, we can indirectly regulate the feeling, which is not. Thus," he explains, "the sovereign voluntary path to cheerfulness, if your cheerfulness be lost, is to sit up cheerfully and to act and speak as if cheerfulness were already there."

The same goes for gratitude. Sit up cheerfully and be grateful. Genuine feelings will follow.

A few years ago, my doctor found a mass of irregular tissue in me - I won't say where. They did a biopsy (I was so brave!) and sent a sample off to see if it was cancerous. That may have been the longest 10 days of my life. It was benign. I immediately set out to celebrate. I got my very first iPhone. I am the only person I know who NEVER had cancer, but has celebrated being cancer free. It was a big deal!

No stress.

I seriously desire to live a stress free life. I have Irritable Bowel Syndrome (IBS). I'm not going to explain that here, but my gastroenterologist says that 50% of all problems I have pertaining to IBS are stress related. So I have a seriously "Down On Stress" campaign going. I recently found a wonderful quote on the *Sole Mates* Website – It states that "Life is too short for matching socks!" So there. Decided. We will choose less stress and more rest! Since my illness I have learned to always make time to rest. Our bodies heal when we are resting, so next time you feel like you are wasting time when you're sitting on the couch, stop! Correct your thinking, and rest! Another activity we need to make time for is dreaming. With dreaming comes creativity and hope. And who doesn't need more hope? My mind needs to be renewed in the truth of the Word of God daily. I may need a perspective shift! Go for it - healthy thinking makes a happy life.

There is a time for everything, says the writer of Ecclesiastes. There is a time to work and a time to play. But let's be quite clear about something. Leisure time is not a time to "check out" of our faith. It is actually a time when we can run to God and delight in Him. If you're going to the Swiss Alps for a holiday, think how wonderful it would be to sing praises to God whilst looking at the mountains and listening to the cowbells? I heard a speaker recently say that recreation actually allows me to be re-created. God, Who makes all things new, makes me new, when I come to Him.

<u>Making life fun.</u>

I love having fun. Don't you? Let's live creatively
and make life fun. In our family we have had
Surprise Cafes, where the menu didn't really
describe the food items properly, so you didn't
know what you were ordering.   I have had picnics in
the middle of the kitchen floor, imagining we were
on a tropical beach somewhere.   I embrace the
freedom of calling myself an "Adventurer" and
where that will take me.   One day my house turned
into a potato factory.   An upside-down tricycle on
the kitchen floor with potatoes lodged in its spokes
and a few pots made a wonderful assembly line, and
the children had never had so much fun. And
sometimes, when you live in Great Britain, you just
have to go to the butchers for a sugar mouse.
Sometimes nothing else will do. There are days
when you need to hang your clothes and bed sheets
on the line so they'll smell like sunshine. Anything
can be fun, no matter what we're doing, whether its
dishes for the family, or singing to a crowd of 5000
people, if we are savouring the moment and doing
it for the glory of God.

<u>Back to basics.</u>

Have you noticed the trend among the Millennials to go back to the basics? I am still playing my old records, because those old Imperials' songs still minister to me. They are now playing vinyl records because they find it charming and want to go back to when life was simpler. I may be on Instagram, Facebook, Snapchat, Twitter, and LinkedIn, while many of them are coming off of social media, because they are wanting to unplug. Interesting? Maybe. It could be that a person's head can only connect with so much for a limited period of time, and it starts to get tired.   Back to basics for some will mean learning to live within their means. It will mean getting rid of credit card debt and the worry that goes along with owing other people money! I'd also like to get back to the basics of relational living. Remember the elderly, who wish they had realized earlier to invest their lives in their children, and that life was not ALL about work! That the state of their RELATIONSHIPS was more important than the state of their homes?

I already know that the happiest people are those who do not live for themselves, but who pour themselves out into others and a purpose bigger than themselves. So, if I follow Christ, and where He leads me, TODAY, will I not be full of joy, find my waking hours full, as well as be useful and a blessing to others?

The Lord has promised to give us the wisdom we need when we ask Him. So, what am I waiting for? I can say, "Lord, I don't know what to do in this situation. Will you show me?" or "I'm so tired, Lord, can you show me what's REALLY important right now, so that I can use the strength that I have for something that is really worthwhile?"

Life can seem so confusing when we have the wrong perspective and the wrong starting point. I'm writing this, to myself, to remind me, that HE is my starting point. When I begin with Him, life makes sense, and I know that everything is going to be okay.

Oh, sweet PEACE . . .

Take a 5-minute break every day to celebrate SOMETHING. You will not have to look hard to find a happy moment or person or thing to celebrate. I know you can. What did you find to celebrate?

_____

_____

_____

Do you regularly make time in your life to Dream?

_____

Can you honestly say, that wherever you are, you are all there? If not, what could you do to help remind yourself to do this? _____

_____

_____

What are your top strengths? Check out www.happify.com to take the quiz. You might be surprised at what you find out about yourself! Simply go to their homepage and click on "My Strengths" to take the assessment!

Life can seem so confusing when we have the wrong
perspective and the wrong starting point. I'm
writing this, to myself, to remind me, that HE is my
starting point. When I begin with Him, life makes
sense, and I know that
everything is going to be okay.

Chapter, the Twenty-fifth.

Thoughts on Marriage.

I'm going to say, right up front, that this is going to be a short chapter. Yes, I love being married, but there are so many fabulous books on marriage out there. I dislike the books that tell me how my husband should be behaving towards me, that is a lose-lose scenario. I expect him to behave a certain way, and then am inevitably disappointed, after reading such a book. In my opinion, the best book on marriage was written in the 1980s, by Anne Ortlund, and is called, *Building a Great Marriage.* I've read many since then, and it's still my all-time favourite!

Some people marry someone quite a bit like themselves. If this is you, then the material covered below may not be that helpful to you. I married someone who is the opposite counterpart of me, in almost every sense of the word. It is my children that have brought this to my attention. Of course.

Wyatt and I were not looking for spouses. First and foremost, we wanted to love and serve the Lord. If He brought someone across our path that we couldn't get around, then we would know it was of God. That's pretty much what happened. We could have lived apart, but did we want to? Well, no. And so the Lord led us together to lead a life of serving Him.

Like many of you, I wanted to be the best wife I could be, and I still want that. In a thirty-one year time span, I've learned a lot. But I always have more to learn. I have learned that I am responsible for myself and my own words and actions. He is responsible for his. We have kind of melted together over the years, and are more similar than we were, but we are still polar opposites. That's not going to change. We find our common places. I have made a list of things that we are really good at doing together, so we can maximize on our strengths. We throw great parties and are great at reaching out to people, both in very different ways, but it works for us. A real highlight in the past few years was getting to do ministry together again, which is what we were doing when we first met. I went back to the UK with my husband and I fell in love with him all over again! We fell in love, being good at doing ministry together, and it was so wonderful to work alongside of him, again. To be reminded of his amazing passion for the lost, his fantastic and practical ideas, and his determination to do whatever it takes.

Years ago, Stormie Omartian wrote a book about praying for your husband called *The Power of a Praying Wife*. I was really challenged by it, back in the 90s. Well, the message was simply this – Make sure you pray for your husband. It matters. Be intentional about it. I was so amazed when I saw God working in my husband's life as I committed to pray for him. One such occasion, I thought that instead of nagging, persistently, I would just pray that he would get around to mowing the back lawn. That very day, he came home from work and mowed the lawn. Why is it that we pray for our husbands and then stand there with our mouths wide open when God answers our prayers? Pray that God will get a hold of your husband's heart. Your husband will be glad that you did. Praying the Word of God is especially effective. I often pray that the Lord would guard my husband's heart, for he is devoted to Him. (Psalm 86:2) I also pray that Wyatt would take good care of my heart, for I am devoted to him.

I am learning that I really need to make an effort to KNOW my man. Did you know that married people are not necessarily kindred spirits? You don't have to be soulmates to create a good marriage and to make it work! Read that sentence again if you need to. Disney presents soulmates as true love. True love happens when you choose to love, no matter what. This is true. I love my husband, even when he loves things I don't, or I love things that he does not love. It's okay. Find your common ground and enjoy that place together. Marriage always works when two people are committed to one another and when divorce or separation is not an option. Marriage works.

I may have to adjust my thinking. I may have thought that my life would look different at this point than it does. It's okay. God's plan is perfect. Forgiveness is so important in any relationship, but especially in marriage. There have been times when I have built a wall around myself, because I don't want to be hurt any more. Walls are never good. If I will just trust my husband's heart, good things will happen. Many times he does not know that he has hurt me. If I trust his heart, and believe that it is never his intention to cause me pain, then we are more than halfway there to a solution, and to staying close. I can't say it enough. Trust his heart.

I have to be so careful how I speak to my husband. He needs me to approve of him, as much as I need him to approve of me! I care about what he thinks of me! So think about the golden rule – I need to treat him, the way I would wish someone to treat me! I need to encourage his heart, as much as I hope he will encourage mine! I want to value his opinion and listen carefully to him when he feels like talking to me. My worst habit is to comment when he shares things with me. I am working on just learning to listen to him, without judgement or comment. Pray for me, please! When I have in the past, commented, I have seen his spirit wither up and crawl away. Watch the spirit of your spouse and tend to it carefully.

A faithful, God fearing man is a rare blessing. I am thankful that my husband loves God more than he loves me. He is a good teacher and has led many people to faith in Jesus Christ. He desires to always follow the Lord's leading in his life. Yes, we get it wrong, so often, but I am thankful that he has never walked out on me. I am thankful that we're in this together until death do us part. I'm thankful that we have a lot of history together, and when life gets hard, we draw closer together, not farther apart. If this is not true, at the moment, in your marriage, then get down on your knees and pray. Your husband needs your prayers. God hears every one, and catches your tears in His bottle. (Read Psalm 56:8)

Remember that you are not alone. Please take a few moments to work through the exercises below.

Think about your spouse. Take a moment to remember why you fell in love with him/her! List some of these reasons here. _____

_____

_____

_____

Can you trust your spouse's heart and believe that he/she is not hurting you on purpose? _____

_____

_____

If your husband ever gets upset or protective, could it be that he just wants to fix and make things right? Can you think of a recent example?

_____

_____

_____

When the Bible says that women are the weaker ones, of course it means physically weaker. Chivalry is not dead. Do you let your husband take care of you? _____

Write down an example of how he tries to take care of you. _____

_____

Let him take care of you, when he tries to.

It will bless you both, I promise.

"You keep track of all my sorrows. You have collected all my tears in your bottle. You have recorded each one in your book."

(Psalm 56:8 - NLT)

Chapter, the Twenty-sixth.

Thoughts on Family.

"Above all, love one another, deeply from the heart; remember that love covers a multitude of sins."

(1 Peter 1:22; 4:8 – paraphrase mine)

This is a huge topic, so I am just going to share my thoughts, dreams and experiences with you. If you find something useful, then I will be thankful that I could share something that I learned with you. We all get a lot of things wrong – we're human, after all. But I believe that family is the most important place to get it right. We've all seen (or maybe done it ourselves) someone put their best foot forward when meeting a stranger, or making that extra effort when meeting a potential boss, for example. I'd like to suggest that how we treat our own families is a real test of character, and a better picture of who we really are.

Let's talk about the importance of belonging. Everyone wants to belong. Songwriters write about it, teenagers search for approval, children act out when they don't get the attention they need. We ALL have this need to belong. When I was growing up, Mom and Dad made each of us feel like we were their favourite. How did they do that? This is a gift that I would seriously like to pass on to my children. We hug and kiss a lot and constantly find pleasure in doing things for each other. Unconditional love. There's something so SAFE about it. To be always welcome, and never sent away. That's what it means to belong.

One of the things my children really missed, being raised on another continent away from our extended families, was this sense of acceptance and belonging – at least of belonging to a larger group than our little family of six. Some of them now want to make up for lost time and others aren't really bothered. Is it possible to get used to that isolated, lonely feeling? Of course, we can join clubs and have hobbies, and get involved in our local churches.   That all helps us to feel like we are living a useful life and have a purpose outside of ourselves and an avenue through which to "give back".

One time, since we've lived in Georgia, my mother and sister, Wendy were able to come and stay with us for a week – what a great time of coffee drinking and game playing! We are so blessed to have families that we wish we could spend MORE time with (I've heard too many stories of families who just don't even like each other – I can't imagine!!)! The distance from our current home to my home town is roughly 3,000 miles, not an easy journey. I try to get back twice a year – basically I am there one month out of every twelve.   Not bad – my lovely family do not begrudge me going away, and are very understanding and let me go happily. I've always told them that I would be a better mummy when I got back, if they let me go away for a little while. I used to leave a teddy bear on my bed, and tell them that they could curl up there, anytime they liked, and could tell Tedderick C. Bear all about it, whatever "it" was.

Somehow, when you are in a family that surrounds you with unconditional love, you can bear any burden. You see the challenges and struggles of life, but you can bear it. Because I grew up with a kind of rock solid stability, I've always wanted to bless my own children with the same. I wanted to make Christmas's amazing, because of the incredible Christmas's that my parents gave to me. I really have nothing to offer my own children but a heart that is devoted to Christ. I want to model His unconditional love for me, for them. What could be more important than unwavering love and a desire to live in peace and harmony?

Developing family time certainly goes against the grain of society. In the age of social media, where family mealtimes are all but gone, we have to plan to create family time, and then fight to keep it. When the children were little, our family times of studying and memorizing the Word of God together at 7 p.m. every evening was a treasure.   We could count on it. And when possible, we would eat together at 6 pm. It's harder now, because everyone has jobs and school, but we try to make it happen whenever it is possible. The way I see it, Mama is the heart of the family, and Daddy is at the helm. I noticed that during my last trip away, the calendar stayed on the date that I left for my trip. When I came home two weeks later, it was still on the same date. Mamas make homes homey. And it's so good for everyone, and makes us feel so safe, when Daddy is at the helm making sure everything is okay.

Children need to experience a lot of life while they are still in the safe environs of a loving home. I always tried to make lots of wonderful opportunities for my children as they were growing. At any one time, we tried not to have more than one paid activity per child per week. We wanted them to have lots of time to play, to create, and to imagine. Over the years, however, our children were involved in many activities. These ranged from children's choirs, voice lessons, water skiing, swimming, fishing, gymnastics, ballet, horse riding, bass playing, drum lessons, Taekwondo, Drama, library visits, National trust homes, long walks, to copious amounts of church activity.

We believed in giving them responsibility. F.W.'s first job was a paper route. He told them he could not work on Sundays, and they talked all about the nice family that had high standards. When they offered him another five days of work, we let him decide and he thankfully turned it down because of his school work. All of our children have been nannies at one time or another – I suppose, because they had such good nannies, and were able to give to other children the loving care that they had been given when they were children. Anne has worked at Christian coffee shops, Frank has worked in several restaurants, Elizabeth has been a Starbucks Barista, and now has her own photography business. They have grown up knowing how to work hard, and I am so proud of every one of them.

What were our priorities as we raised our family? Well, whether other people agreed with us or not, we put God first. We believed that when God called us into ministry that He also called our children into ministry. God created the family. If He called us, so clearly, into ministry, then we had to believe that it was the right place for them to be, as well. You have no doubt heard people talking about the irresponsibility of parents who would take their children into the jungle of Papua New Guinea. If they're following God, then there are no worries that God can't handle. Some of the most beautiful people I have ever met were once children raised in a jungle somewhere. There where they have not been corrupted by the craze for materialism, and the need for status and power. They care about people and understand what is really important.

So yes, serving God is number one. We can serve God together, right? You would always find us in ministry before you would ever find us at a baseball game or ballet recital for our kids. Yes, we did the recitals and games, but they never came before our commitment to the Body of Christ. We just always tried to make sure that our personal pleasure never kept us from serving God. In fact, **we found our personal pleasure in serving God.** If this is foreign to you and it sounds strange, just understand that to me, our children's characters were more important than their achievements. We have failed in many ways, as parents, but these were our goals and desires, and I'm so thankful to God for leading us every step of the way. We have learned that it is only possible to live a happy, satisfied life when we are loving our God and putting Him first. It is far too easy to make parenting about us – the parents. I even remember one of my children saying to me, "This is not about you. Don't try to make it about you." I guess that's what we do, when we are caring more about our reputation, our standing in society, or our appearance to others, than about what is really best for our children.

This is the hardest chapter I have written so far. To declare what my goals and desires have been. To know what is right, and to do my best, even though I know how often I have failed. I don't want to sound at all arrogant or proud of these high goals that the Lord gave me. I feel very exposed and know that I may be judged. I tell myself that it's okay. Life is hard and good at the same time. I don't want to miss anything that God has for me, by not reaching high enough! I used to say to my kids, when I dressed them – "Reach for the Stars!" – well, I want to do that too.

One thing my parents modelled for me was to be happy to serve one another. Hebrews 10:24 says, "Let us outdo one another in love and good deeds." (paraphrase mine)   I grew up in a home where people were happy to help each other. I would simply mention something about needing to get some ironing done, and my Dad had set up the ironing board for me before I had even got up out of my chair! When I lost my favourite hat, I remember my older sister driving miles to buy me another one. I remember my brother grinding fresh coffee for me to enjoy the next morning. I remember sitting around a fire pit, with as many of the family as could gather, laughing and sharing stories. My daughter Anne has often put a hot water bottle into my bed before I got there, knowing that I was tired and ill, and that it would help me. Sometimes just offering to give someone a lift, emptying a full dishwasher, or a kind card on my pillow at night show love. I guess if my family has taught me anything, it is to stop complaining, and to start serving with a joyful heart. When I am blessed by someone's kindness, I want to reach out, in turn, and show kindness to someone else!   My kids will certainly catch the example far more than any lecture!

I loved having a house full of little ones.   Four children under eight was like heaven to me. Mondays were like Saturdays to us, because it was Wyatt's day off. We would go to Kew Gardens, Broxted Hill Farm, or Kensington Gardens. It was so FUN just to have my babies all around me. I learned to encourage good behaviour instead of jumping all over the bad behaviour.   Yes, we dealt with the vice, but focused on the virtue! My preschool teacher training was a tremendous preparation for this. Instead of saying, "Don't get out of bed," I learned to say, "Please obey mummy and stay in your bed." Focus on the positive! They wanted to please us! We taught them to fold their hands to help them to be self-controlled. They would put their hands on our arms when they needed us, instead of interrupting us with their words.   We taught

Elizabeth and Heather to use sign language by nine months of age, and it was wonderful to see how much less frustrated they were, because they could communicate with us. I taught my children how to read (sometimes with the help of our wonderful nannies), we did home school together, we made play-doh and cookies, painted the back fence with water, and made old fashioned pull taffy. Life was fun. One evening, I called up to F.W. to say goodnight to him. He called back - "Come upstairs Mummy – I'd like to see your beautiful face!" What a charmer. One day Elizabeth said, "I'm glad that mummies don't go away like nannies do!" I was blessed to be able to stay home with my children. I'm just so thankful.

Now, raising teenagers, was more of a challenge to me. I wanted to laugh, kiss and hug often, but sometimes they didn't feel like it. I realized that I had not been given the job of being the children's BUDDY, but rather their parent, guide, and teacher. I sat beside a lovely Italian girl on an overseas flight one day. She asked about my children, and when I told her that we were becoming good friends, she reacted quite strongly. She said that children only have one mother, and that she needs to continue to be the mother that they need. Her passion about this made a lasting impression on me. I realized that it is easy to feel bullied by your children's emotions, but that no matter how desperate they may be, I must remember that I am the grown-up here, and that they need me to be the grown-up. I also realized that sometimes I would parent out of fear instead of with courage and backbone! Doing things together with teens certainly helped a lot. I remember sitting with F.W. while he did his algebra. We actually laughed and had a good time. Why does it not surprise me that he is graduating with a major in accounting soon? I have never enjoyed math, but it wasn't about that. It was about building a relationship with my son.

Every day, I would ask the Lord to make me a minister of His peace, literally. I learned that it is important to choose my battles wisely. I would ask myself, "Is this worth making a federal case out of it?"

And finally, instead of lecturing, I tried to say,

"What happened here? And what do you need to do to make it right?"

This hopefully helped them to process moral truth, and to come to the right decision themselves. If they worked it out on their own, I figured it might be a lasting lesson.

What about husbands and sons? Yes, no matter what the media says, they are different than the female of the human race. Really. I was once told by a wise friend that when talking to husbands or sons, keep it short, don't spin a web. And don't we girls love to spin webs? Putting on respect for my husband and my son really works. They respond so well. Now if I could just remember this every day of my life, I'd be doing great!

You work hard to build a family that is close and loving and sometimes it doesn't seem to be going too well. The song, *All About Love*, by Steven Curtis Chapman says,

---

Now they're fighting in the Middle East
And they're fighting down on 7th street
And there are fights
In my own house on given days

It's like something's lurking deep inside
That can't seem to be satisfied
But life was not meant
To be lived this way

Cause it's true for every man

And woman, every boy and girl

That our only hope for living

Here together in this world

Is love, love, love, love, love.

It's all about Love.

So, imagine how I felt one night, when I came home after days of sibling wars, and F.W. and Elizabeth were actually hugging one another. Who says miracles don't happen???!!!

When my dad & Wyatt's father passed away exactly three weeks apart, it happened so fast that it hardly seemed real. What did I take away from that very difficult time? That every day is precious. To live well today, because we don't know what tomorrow will bring. Love our families, and those who are placed in our path while it is still today. And I learned that the Lord God is strong enough to carry me through ANYTHING.

How can I wrap up this most difficult chapter? I guess by being brutally honest. You can read all the parenting and marriage books out there, but you still have to figure it out in your own personal situation. Where exactly is the freedom for a parent to learn and change and grow? You've never been a parent before and you have to learn as you go. We've never done this before, right? We need wisdom to know how hard to push our children to be the best they can be. And the wisdom to know how hard is too hard. Let's be really gracious towards one another on this path we call life. I probably could not walk in your shoes and live your life, and you probably would not want to live mine. Everybody is working through something. Let's be kind to one another.

Sure, life is hard. But it is good. Don't miss noticing the Hand of God everywhere you look, in every day that you live. Now it's time for the application!

Take a moment to acknowledge that sometimes life is very hard. It's ok to say it.

Now take a moment to realize that life is also good. Make a list of some of the blessings in your life, right now. _____

_____

_____

_____

_____

_____

_____

Sometimes it is easy to be judgmental of the way others parent. We tend to judge what we have no experience of or don't understand. Let's admit that we don't know everything. Let's stop judging each other and start encouraging each other, to follow the Lord and to be the best we can be in all of our relationships!

Can you think of any ways in which you find yourself being judgemental of other parents? _____

_____

_____

_____

Write down one way that you can encourage a
parent you know, this week. They will be glad you
did! _____

_____

_____

_____

We all get a lot of things wrong – we're human, after
all. But I believe that family is the most important
place to get it right.

Chapter, the Twenty-seventh.

Learn from the Smallest of These.

In my lifetime, I have been greatly influenced by Francis and Edith Schaeffer (philosopher, teacher and authors), as well as the writings of their daughter, Susan S. Macaulay. Mrs. Macaulay wrote an exceptional book called, *For the Children's Sake.* If a person could only read one book (besides the Bible, of course) to help them in their parenting, then I would suggest that this is the book! In it she taught that children are born people. Sounds obvious, but think about it this way - that even in infancy, they have things to teach us, and that we should learn what we can from them, and recognize the privilege of learning from them. So many adults think that it's all about what we have to teach the children! This is so erroneous. Children are made in the image of God, and therefore reflect His likeness. I believe we would do well to watch and learn from them. I always tell my music students that I expect to learn far more from them than they could ever learn from me. And I believe it. I, of course, am not suggesting that children are perfect. I AM suggesting that they reflect some of the beauty of the Lord, and that we would do well to learn from them.

Jesus said to let the children come to Him. They are precious and the faith that they are capable of is beautiful. When we talk about the faith of a child, we basically mean to have a faith that has no room for doubt. Isn't that true? Children are also capable of such selfless beauty. Wanting what is best for someone else, without calculating what they will get out of it. I am committed to learning what I can from the children in my life. I hope you will choose to do the same.

I'm just going to take a moment to tell you a little more detail about the precious children that the Lord gave to Wyatt and me.

Anne Sherridan was born in 1990. She was named after Wyatt's mother, Ann Gwin, although we added the "e" to her name, because of my passion for the writings of L.M. Montgomery, author of *Anne of Green Gables*. We named her Sherridan after my very wonderful Canadian friend, Sherridan Reimer (nee Klaassen). Anne and I had a special relationship because when she was born, she had me all to herself. We did everything together. She has a caring, tender heart and a beautiful smile on her face for everyone she sees. One evening, when she was four or five, I was too ill to lift myself off of the couch. I also had two smaller children, so she very helpfully took charge of the situation, and offered to make the two little babies some supper. I remember very clearly, her standing on a chair and reaching the bag of potato chips (crisps) off the top of the fridge.   Many times, she took it upon herself to undress me and put me to bed when I had no one else to help me. When people came to visit, she would offer them a seat and a glass of water. She told them NOT to sit on the couch, because mama needed to lay there. If I want a gripping conversation, I talk with Anne. We both love museums and read copious amounts of books. I loved teaching her to read at the age of five and preparing her for her testimony at the age of seven, when she was baptized.   What a brave girl she was! I don't know many other seven-year-olds who would get up in front of an entire congregation to share a three-minute testimony! We tried to take holidays where we could learn and grow as Christians, as well as get away from the city. I particularly remember our weeks at Grace Family Bible Camp in Cornwall. On one particular occasion, Anne went forward for prayer at a morning meeting. I so desperately wanted to go to her, but decided not to, in case she would have preferred someone else! Wyatt leaned over and whispered, "Go to her," which confirmed to me that I should. It was lovely. The Lord showered us with His grace, and we felt His power. It had been years since I had cried or prayed like that. What a blessing. I was almost too aware of giving her an opportunity to talk to someone else, that I very nearly missed that amazing moment in our history together. What do I continue to learn from Anne? That it is important to be aware of the feelings of others, a lot about psychology, endless information about cats and fairy tales, and what is considered to be a healthy vegetarian diet.

Frank Wyatt IV was born in 1992. As you can tell from his name, he was the fourth in a succession of Franks. On the delivery table we decided to call him F.W. Frank, with his deep, booming voice, as a toddler, was such an incredible mixture of funny and serious, that I never knew which to expect at any given moment. One day while we were sitting on the couch after family Bible study time one night, Frank touched my bare leg and said, "Mama, you have too many calories in your legs!" Yeah, well. Once when we picked him up at the nursery at church, he burst loudly into song, "Lovely weather for a sleigh ride together with you!"   That's right, F.W. Keep me laughing. One day he came home asking if I would support him, if he started leading a Bible Study at our house, once a week, for the younger teens. I was so happy that the Lord was working in his life in such amazing ways. I remember the day that our dear neighbour, George, came to our front door to tell Frank that God can do anything. With tears in his eyes, he reminded us to trust God, with whatever we were facing at the moment.   F.W. was wanting to go to Bible College in Canada, and we did not yet have the money. It was such a great faith lesson for him. God used another friend to provide, and he did head off to college that fall, but how wonderful to see God work in that wonderful way. Frank is tender hearted, passionate, yet logical and cool headed. What do I learn from Frank? That it's good to laugh. That it's good to do my work first and then play later. And that meaningful conversations are possible with teenage boys.

Elizabeth Walker was born in 1994. "Elizabeth" was Wyatt's mother's middle name, and Walker was my mother's maiden name. Because I fell ill when she was only a few months old, Elizabeth never remembers me feeling good. She was born a charmer and made friends wherever she went. When very little, F.W. decided to call her Biff, and so she is to this day. She was a very contented child. She was the first child I had, after doing a *Growing Kids God's Way* course, by Gary and Anne Marie Ezzo, which was a huge paradigm shift for me. Elizabeth talked with her hands, was always happy and smiley, and everyone loved her. When she was one and a half years old we took her Christmas shopping to Toys R Us. She saw a bear on the shelf, picked her up, and would not let the bear out of her sight. Ever. Yes, I paid for her and because it was Christmas, she was named Holly. Biff's ears were wonky at birth and she was so brave to have surgery on her ears while still very young. Of course, the play nurse at the hospital had to operate on Holly's ears too, which I hasten to say, was a great success. Elizabeth likes to please people, and seems to like to learn things the hard way. She is personable, charming, and an artist by nature. She sings beautifully and is also quite the photographer. She has helped to teach me to savour life. Every minute of it.

Heather Katheryn was born in 1997. I was still very ill, but we made a conscious decision to trust God, and go ahead and have another baby. We are so glad that the Lord filled us with faith at this difficult time in our lives, Otherwise, we would not have our precious Heather. Poor Heather was nameless for three whole weeks after she was born. The name we chose had to be perfect because she was amazing from the moment she was born with her cleft palate, and later with her pyloric stenosis issues. We named her Heather, in the end, because she was strong and hardy, like the wild Scottish heather flower. I remember, after her palate surgery, that she was so brave and resilient. She was nine months old, and had no thought for how amazing she was, or how pitiable she was! She just got on with whatever life seemed to throw at her. When she was two years old, she helped me to carry cleaning supplies to the shed. She had a wonderful time lining them up. In her mind, the toilet cleaner was talking to the carpet powder, and the disinfectant was talking to the kitchen cleaner. "Let's get rid of the toys," I thought. She was so happy and content, sitting on the floor, arranging all the bottles around her. When we lived in Wales, we had a big lovely yard, with an ancient stone wall around it. I remember waking up one morning to Heather pounding on the window. Her friend had been outside playing since 6:30 a.m. and she wanted to go outside and play too. She has an outgoing personality and loves people. She watches people and learns about them.   What has Heather taught me?   That anything is possible. Along with her cleft palate, she had a Pierre Robin chin – which basically means she was born without one. I believe it was a miracle that it grew for her. Many times it does not, and more surgery is required. She has also taught me to be brave, and reminded me many times that my relationship with the Lord is the most important thing in my life. I would ask her to empty the dishwasher for example, and she would agree to do it, as soon as she finished her Bible reading and Quiet Time. Thanks Heather for modelling a passion for Christ.

I was often reminded while raising the children, about Samuel's mother. She told the Lord that if He gave her a child, that she would give that child back to God. With the help of the Lord, that's what I wanted to do. For His glory and the sake of His

Name.   When the children were little I would run away to meet with the Lord in my room. Once in there, I would put a scarf on the doorknob, which I explained to the children was a sign that I was not to be disturbed, because I was praying for them!   I would hear them standing outside of my door and whispering. "We can't knock. She's praying for us. Leave her alone, F.W." said Anne, "She'll be out soon."

The ultimate presupposition for working with and training my children every day was this: To Love the Lord our God with all our hearts and to love our neighbour as ourselves. *(Luke 10:27 – paraphrase mine)* (Wyatt and I wanted to get to the hearts of our children with moral truth.

What about other people's children?   Oh yes, I want to learn from them also. I take regular lessons on what the latest apps are from all the kids in my life.   I learn from what social media they are on, and about what matters to them, socially. They are growing up with devices and therefore know the current code of social behaviours better than anyone.   When talking to children of all ages, I like to ask them questions to find out what matters to them. I talk to them as people, not as immature children. The whole point of writing this is to simply say that no matter if we are hanging out with a one-year-old, or an 89-year-old, there is always something that we can learn from others.

Now it's time for a little introspection. I do hope that you are making time to answer these personal questions. No one can answer them but you!

Do you have the faith of a child? A faith that has no room for doubt? _____

_____

What are you needing to trust God with? Ask God for the faith of a child. _____

_____

_____

Do you have the attitude that children can teach you something? Don't miss this. _____

_____

Chapter, the Twenty-eighth.
Thoughts on Friendships.

Because I am so busy at home, I don't seem to have a lot of time to just 'walk' this life with many other people. Boy, am I thankful to the Lord for the Praise Team at church. We may not always have time to talk deeply about things, but we are walking this road together, and that's so good. I pray for opportunities to get close to people, but there's just not a lot of time. I'm not complaining, just wondering if this is just my space in life right now. When the kids were little, I did SO much with other people. Because of my illness, I have to sleep a lot too, and that seems like such a waste of time for someone who loves to be busy, like I do. Am I ever thankful for my feather duvet and comfortable bed! God has been so good to us. My electric kettle is boiling right now, to make another cup of tea, and to fill a hot water bottle.

Some people are blessed to have Godly older women in their lives, all the way through. The Lord sent me just who I needed, to learn certain things, and then they were gone, either because they had to move on or because I did. It's like the Lord just wanted me to have them in my life for a season but not learn to really rely on them. He wants me to trust only HIM. But aren't friendships great? I believe that even the most introverted person needs some social interaction in their life – to have someone who will take the time to really listen and to look into other people's eyes. That's the only way to see their soul, right? When you look into someone's eyes, a connection happens.

What about when people are not easy to be friendly with? That's when I pray for them. I actually have learned that when someone does not seem to like me very much, that I make it my prayer challenge to pray for them. Some of my best friends have come out of this. If I had not prayed for these women, I would have totally missed out on some amazing friendships! Some of the hardest characters have been softened through the resilience of regular prayer and a few kind words here and there.

I thank God for the friends who have stuck with me, across the continents, and throughout the years.

We cannot rely on one another on a day to day basis, but when we get back together, it's like we have never been apart. You know who you are, and how much I love you and value all of your prayers, and the input you have had in my life over the years. What really makes a person who they are? We learn so much from so many people, that we often forget who taught us what, but we need to remember that we did not become who we are today by growing and teaching ourselves. We are God's workmanship, created in Christ Jesus to do good works. *(Ephesians 2:10 – paraphrase mine)* He moulds us, as a potter moulds clay on a wheel, to make us useful for His purposes. Let's remember humility and to thank God for all the people who have poured into our lives, to make us into who we are today, for His glory.

Because of my illness, people have many times wanted more from me than I had the ability to give them. I try to be honest and hope they will understand, but some have walked away. I have to trust God with those, and let them go. It's okay. Maybe in this 21st century, we are learning that we can only be intimately close with a certain number of people, even if we know thousands and are "friends" with them on Facebook. Wisdom is needed here.

Always leave your friends wishing they had had more time with you. When our children were little, we used to say, "IT'S NEVER LONG ENOUGH!" but hey, better to leave them wanting more right? An old adage from my parent's day is "Never over-stay your welcome." Of course that comes right from the Bible – Don't let your foot be often in your neighbour's house! *(Proverbs 25:17 – paraphrase mine)* They will tire of you! We used to go to visit my elderly great grandparents on a Sunday afternoon. A mom, a dad, five children, and a rather large dog, would take up their entire living room. When my Grandpa Newbury had had enough, he would get up and wind the clock on his mantelpiece. That was our cue to say our goodbyes. Remember, it's always better to leave people wishing that they could have spent MORE time with you!

People often define friendships quite differently. Your definition for friendship may be quite different than mine. *The English Oxford Living Dictionary*, however, states that a friend is a person whom one knows and with whom one has a bond of mutual affection, typically exclusive of sexual or family relations. We can broaden and explain this definition with synonyms from a thesaurus. A friend may fall into the category of a companion, a soul mate, an intimate, a confidant, a second self, a playmate, a classmate, or a workmate. Some people would say if you find one good friend in the world, that you are blessed indeed, and others would have a much looser definition, and say that friends are people who you hang out with. Sometimes friendships are formed around hobbies and interests. Some friends you laugh with, some friends give you really good advice. One thing that everyone may agree on however is that friendship must be mutual to really be a friendship. Being friendly is one thing. Being friends might perhaps be something altogether different.

A few years ago the women at our church enjoyed a fabulous weekend away. Besides working on our relationships with one another, our souls were fed deeply on the Word of God. We learned about *'LOVING WELL'* and how it all starts with letting the Lord love me deeply; or rather, letting Him into my life and experiencing His amazing love. We talked about how we can get so busy serving and loving others, that we don't take time to feel how loved we are. **And every woman knows that if she doesn't feel loved, in her marriage or in any other**

relationship, it's harder to express love to others. So, I was reminded that I am so deeply loved by the Lord. By the way – so are you!

There are those in our world that have seen so much of the ugly side of life, that they find it really hard to believe that there is goodness to be found. Our experience is that we often find what we're looking for. We are all sinful people who get it wrong sometimes, but I want to search and find the good in people. Edith Schaeffer, in her book *Forever Music* called it "Left-over Beauty". We were made in God's image, but even after Adam and Eve sinned in the garden, and experienced "the Fall," there is still lots of leftover beauty in all of God's creations! Let's be good finders, instead of fault finders! Sometimes I think it's like a treasure hunt – you know there's a good quality in that person somewhere, but you're having a hard time seeing it!!

Many people are generous. So many times, our needs have been meet perfectly without the giver even knowing of our need. I believe God just puts something on a heart, a way to give perhaps, or a way that they can be helpful, so that every need will be met. Of course there are other times when people have given us specific items we needed – a kitchen table, a house to live in while in the US, or some furniture to fill our house when we moved back to the States. God's people are GENEROUS. I remember once not having enough money to buy groceries, and coming home only to find a bag of groceries left on our doorstep. God wants us to be the answer to someone's prayers. If we are God's people, we need to hear His voice and look for opportunities to be generous.

And one last thought. Friendship isn't about me and my needs. We have had so many hundreds of people come through our home that we may never see again. We treated these people like they were friends, and took the opportunities to pour into their lives what they were in need of. Perhaps encouragement, perhaps a hearty meal. It could be that when God brings people across our paths, it's to show them how much HE loves them. I don't want to miss a single opportunity to be a part of what God is doing.

Hebrews 13:2 says, "Do not forget to show hospitality to strangers, for by so doing some people have shown hospitality to angels without knowing it." (NIV)

Who knows whom we might have the opportunity to meet today?

Think of someone you would consider a dear friend. Thank them somehow for that friendship today. How will you reach out to them today? _____

_____

Think of someone whom you regularly see, that you aren't particularly close to, for one reason or another. Pray for that person today. Write your prayer so you'll remember to thank God when He answers! _____

_____

_____

Now take a few minutes to meditate on the love of God for you. The Psalmist says again and again, that His love is everlasting. Let God fill your heart. When your heart is full, you'll find it easy to give to others!

Chapter, the Twenty-ninth.

Letting go of our pride.
Thankfulness.

Pride has landed the human race in more trouble than any other quality. Remember back to the Garden of Eden, when Satan suggested that Adam and Eve would have their eyes opened and that they would be like God, knowing good and evil, if they ate of the fruit God had forbidden? They probably thought, "What could possibly be wrong about knowing good and evil?" And who wouldn't aspire to be like God? We are fallen in nature, and cannot always trust our human reasoning. Think of the pride that Satan had here. To declare that it was possible to be like God?! Really? We are the created, and He is the Creator. How dare we?

Yet we assume this kind of pride often. We show pride when we think of ourselves more highly than we should. I believe that there is a thankfulness that leads to productivity. We can be thankful to others in our lives who have made certain things possible for us. We can be thankful to others who have gone out of their way to pour into our lives, and open doors of opportunity for us. I must admit, in the real world, I have more often seen people take whatever other people will give them and go on, without thankfulness, crediting themselves for the breaks that they have had, or the success they have enjoyed. We may have gone out of our way to give someone the "break" that they needed, and they have hardly noticed at all. They credit themselves with all of their success, without so much as a look backwards.

People say, "You should be so proud of yourself." Yes, this is okay, if it is not carried too far. When I did well on an exam in high school, I did well because I studied, I worked hard and I knew the material. So yes, I did the right things and I was rewarded by being on the honour roll. But think about all the others involved in this simple scenario. I had teachers who taught well, parents who encouraged me to get enough sleep and eat well, friends with whom I studied, and just the fact that I lived in a country that valued education, and that I had the opportunity to attend school! I should not be proud of myself for any of these things that I had nothing to do with. I need to be thankful to God and these people for opening these doors for me. I am so blessed. This idea kind of goes back to the teamwork chapter. Sometimes we just need to let go of our pride and realize that we are seriously better together than we would be on our own. If a researcher wants all the credit for his scientific findings, he may want to be very private and not share his ideas with anyone. But could he not get much more done in his field if he let go of his pride and let go of getting all the credit, and began to share his ideas and work with others?

Anyone who is really successful in anything has had a team of people around them, cheering them on, and encouraging them in their work. We must realize that who we are is not a product of our own invention. God has made us, placed us in certain places, around certain people, and so many people have poured into our lives. Let's be realistic and be thankful to those people who have helped us in our lives. We tend to idolize people and put them on pedestals. It comes from our innate desire to worship someone or something. So next time we see someone do really well at something, remember that probably many people around them sacrificed in one way or another to bring this about. And ultimately it is God who gives all good gifts. This brings us back to thankfulness again.

Nobody has it all right. There are people who follow John Wesley, or John Calvin or Charles Spurgeon, for example. They were just men! They were godly men, whom the Lord used, but did they have it all right? Of course not. I enjoy their writings about what God had taught them, but they didn't understand everything either. Anyone who thinks they understand it all is arrogant and possibly unteachable. God is outside of any man-made box that we try to devise, because we are trying so hard to understand something. We need to be aware that sometimes we are not able to see things clearly. In I Corinthians 13, Paul said, "We see as through a glass darkly, but then face to face; now I know in part, but then shall I know fully, as I am fully known." (KJV) This is also true in the grey areas of the Christian life. There are somethings that we have not had any experience of, so we create our standards, and then proceed to judge others by our own set of rules. How I want to be kind to others. I may never understand, or have to walk through what their life has given to them, so the need to be humble, and say that I don't understand, is crucial, even though I may be trying to understand.

I want to be thankful to those who work so hard in full time ministry. Their job is hard and will never end, as long as there are people in this world who need their help. This lesson is indelibly printed on my heart. When I was saved, as a girl of six, at an after-school meeting, there was a special guest speaker that day. The local church had invited him in to do after-school magic shows, through which he would share the gospel of Jesus Christ to a room full of children. Twelve years after this event, I was attending Peace River Bible Institute. Of course I had had opportunity to tell my story to people on campus that I was getting to know. One evening, my music teacher phoned me in the dormitory and asked if I could come over to her home. I went immediately, and she introduced me to a Reverend Funk. She had heard my story, and Mr. Funk's story, and put the pieces together. He had been preaching the day that I had put my faith in Christ. He was the magician! I was thrilled to be able to thank him in person for the huge impact that he had had on my life. What if he had not taken that week of ministry at Peace Arch Baptist Church that week when I was six years old? The tears of joy he shed that night at seeing some of the fruit of his labours was life changing for me. It was important to be thankful. I am not who I am because I am some super person, who just always makes all the right choices, and am naturally good. Oh no. Many, many people have poured into my life. That calls me to humility.

God wants to give us good gifts. He is a good, good Father. If we ask for something that is NOT good for us, we need to be thankful that (in His mercy) He does not give us those things!   He is also teaching me to give Him all of my expectations. Seriously, do I deserve anything?   Contrary to what the world says, no, I don't deserve anything.   I am a blessed girl. And it is all God's doing. A perfect example of this is my sweet Elizabeth's wedding. For various reasons at the time, I was not able to really help her with her wedding preparations.   I remember staying up all night, crying out to God, and giving back to Him any rights I thought I deserved. I learned to CHOOSE to thank God for every blessing that comes my way, but not think that I deserve that blessing!   When you ask my husband how he is doing, he may answer, "Better than I deserve."   This is so true.   Any goodness in us is all of God, and we need to give up our rights and expectations of how and what our lives are going to look like. Yes we dream and imagine what our lives may look like. Well, maybe God has something better. And what I need to do is to open my eyes so that I won't miss it.

Sometimes things that once held great meaning and value no longer have usefulness. It's okay to let those things go. How many church stories have we heard over the years of people saying, "Well, we've always done it this way," or "we've never done it that way before." If a tradition or practice has outlived its usefulness, it's okay to be thankful for John Smith, who bought that vase for the front of the church, and to say that we enjoyed it for so many years. And then we can let it go. I had a Lonely Socks Club for years. After many years of faithful service, I have finally disbanded my Lonely Sock Club. It served the purpose of helping me to find matching socks (that invariably get lost in the wash), and also taught my children to match socks. Now my kids are grown. If a practice is no longer useful, then let it go! Be thankful for its usefulness in your life and move on.

And while we're talking about people's pride, we don't have to have it all together all the time. Even some of the time. This is what the Baby Boomers can learn from the Millennials - that our lives don't have to look perfect, because anyone who lives longer than 20 years max, knows that they are not, so why pretend? I remember the first home that Wyatt and I shared in the United States. The cockroaches would come out when the lights went off. The couch in our living room was mouldy somewhere deep inside, and I had to spray it with air freshener before anyone came over. And the worst instance of pride, if you can picture this, was me stuffing all of the dirty dishes into the oven before guests came over because I wanted our home to be picture perfect. I am so thankful to be over this! Now I know that people are coming to see <u>me</u>, and not my house, and it is no longer a pride issue. But how many years did it take me to learn that lesson?

If you EVER think you've got problems, I suggest you hang out in a children's hospital. Your life will never be the same. I've spent so many weeks in children's hospitals, and have been completely humbled by the kind souls I have met there. I have seen so many parents struggling, and so many children being brave. There are so many nurses and doctors really CARING about people. I want to live the rest of my life on earth being REAL. Not pretending in any area of my life, but rather sharing my struggles and victories to help others with theirs.

An absolute favourite chorus of mine is Paul Oakley's *Jesus, Lover of My Soul.* Some of the words go like this,

"It's all about You, Jesus. And all this is for You.

For Your glory and Your fame. It's not about me.

Or that You should do things my way.

You alone are God, and I surrender to Your ways."

It's time to engage with the Lord. As you read through the thoughts and questions below, lay your heart open before God. He is waiting for you.

Ever get tired of the stress of living? Ever just wished you could just die and go to heaven? Remember this - We don't have to live a picture perfect life. We just have to stay close to Jesus. Write your thoughts. _____

_____

_____

_____

Is there any area of your life in which you are harbouring pride?   Any area in which you pride yourself for achieving something single-handed? Acknowledge it.   Then list the people who have helped you in that area, to get to where you are now. _____

_____

_____

_____

_____

And lastly, how can you choose to be authentic and real in your life today?   It could be going to the grocery store without your make-up or it could be sharing a personal struggle with another person.

_____

_____

_____

_____

Chapter, the Thirtieth.

Living well.   Learning from the Best.

It is very interesting to me to notice who has the power to make the most difference in our lives. I believe that the people who make the most difference in our lives are those who we have respect for and those who truly care about us. Occasionally a stranger can walk across our path and have an impact in our lives, but that is only if they are in the right place, at the right time, saying the right thing. It happens. People give us a smile when we need it most, or preach a sermon, or teach a lecture. We don't know them, and they don't know us, but we needed what they had to offer, in that moment. Usually however, it is those that we respect or love that make the biggest impact on our lives long-term.

Sometimes I feel like a fighter and victor in every area of my life, but in my closest relationships. It's because these relationships tend to be the hardest.

These people are the ones who really know us – our good and bad habits, and yet somehow, we care more about what the people closest to us think, than anyone. When people closest to us speak their minds, we can easily get the stuffing knocked out of us. I think that's because we know that these people are the most important. These are the people who will still be there when everyone else has moved on. People may say that they don't care if their daddy is proud of them, but we all know the truth. Children are desperate for their father's approval. And this goes for all close relationships, to a degree. Somehow we feel the need to believe that the people who know us best approve of us.

I am so very thankful for the closest people in my life who have always cheered me on. People who said, "YOU CAN DO IT." My parents fit this description perfectly. I know of no two other people who jointly said, "If you decide to do this thing, we will be 100% behind you." My mother has been an inspiration to me. Years ago, at eighty, she still had so much to give. I could see the depth of love in my mother's eyes and no matter how much I tried to give to her, she always gave MORE. Her spirit is alive, vibrant, and energetic. Dad always told us we could do anything we set our minds to doing. And he believed it. This has been my example from birth.

I've learned that it does matter who I surround myself with. If I surround myself with godly people who are pressing into those good passions, always wanting to be the best they can be, then I will be inspired to be better than I am! How do I live my life when no one is looking? If the walls of my house could talk, what would they tell you? Who I am when nobody is looking matters. When I'm honest and good in the little things, it WILL show up in the big things. And remember, the Bible says, "be sure that your sin will find you out."(Number 32:23 - NIV) If you're hiding something, somebody, sometime, somewhere is going to find out about it. It matters.

How can I be better tomorrow than I am today? Well, of course I need to stay close to Jesus. What is He calling me to do? How do I learn to do that thing WELL, that God is calling me to do? The best way, I have discovered, is to find someone that does it WELL and copy them. You can make it your own style later. For today, copy and learn from the best! I remember being 20 and asked to sing at my church. I chose to sing Amy Grant's *El Shaddai*, which was on the charts at the time. I studied the style of Amy Grant. I copied her every nuance. I was rewarded by being told I sounded just like her THAT DAY singing THAT SONG. I never forgot that lesson. Everything in life has to be learned and there is always someone who can do it better than we can. Whether you want to open a Bed and Breakfast or start an *Etsy* shop online, learning tools are available. Today, with *YouTube* and the internet, there are no excuses not to learn from the best.

Throughout my 55 years, there have been countless number of people who have poured themselves into my life to teach and guide me. My mother was intentional about teaching me to love the written word. My dad was intentional to teach me music. My school music teacher, Mr. Summers, spent hours honing my clarinet skills, taught me to arrange music for the band, and then let the band play my arrangement. I had sewing teachers, French teachers, cooking teachers, Social Studies teachers, all who had a significant input into who I am today. My pastors, youth leaders and college Bible study leaders mentored me spiritually all along the path. My husband has also been a great teacher to me. He has always seemed larger than life to me, and the dreams that God has given him have been bigger than ours ever could have been. I cannot record here all the ways that I have seen God use Wyatt's passion for the Truth and for lost souls for

His glory. Wyatt has helped so many people, and taught and inspired so many others, and I know he inspires me to love the Lord more every day.

Every host family that ever hosted me while I had five years of travel with music groups, choir tours and mission trips, taught me how to offer hospitality to others. Some lessons are just caught, as we watch the excellent example of others. Some lessons are taught very intentionally by the teacher. I've talked about my Edmonton relatives, who were concerned about my spiritual well-being. They always asked me how I was doing, had me come to stay, took me out for lunch and showed genuine interest in me. My Gramma Hall would spend time watching clouds with me, she would play games with me, and she let me help her at the "Over-Sixty" Salvation Army group in Edmonton. There is something so powerful and life-changing about a grownup taking time to show interest in a young person. People like camp counsellors, the staff at my Bible college, a random Wednesday night missionary who taught a song I have never forgotten.

Don't EVER underestimate the influence you can have in someone else's life. You may never know about it, but it matters.

God is my Teacher.   He is the Ultimate Teacher. I am convinced that only by staying in His Word, and by applying His Truth to my life, can I live fully the life that He intended for me.   His dreams for me are so much bigger and greater than my own. At this point, I have to cry out to Him and say, "I have wasted so much time," either just living for myself or not always paying attention to what the Lord would want me to do.

Lord, have mercy on us.

Here are a few practical ways to help you adjust your thinking about how God has used other people in your life in the past, and how He may want to use them in your life in the days to come.

Take time to list here some people who have poured themselves into your life.

_____

_____

_____

_____

_____

_____

Take a few moments to thank one of them for being
such a great influence in developing who you are
today. Email, phone or a nice card – whatever
you're most comfortable with.   How will you thank
someone today?

_____

_____

What is a skill you want to improve? Who can you
learn from, or what resource can you use to improve
in this area?

_____

_____

_____

_____

It matters.

Chapter, the Thirty-first.

Learning perpetually.

"For in Him we live, and move, and have our being".

(Acts 17:28 – NIV)

From knowing so many amazing people in my own life, I have asked myself what makes them so incredible? One fine theme that seems to run through each life is their desire to keep learning and never stop. One of the reasons that we home-educated our children was to show them that learning was not an event that ends at graduation, for example, but that it is absolutely a way of life. We should be learning and desiring to learn from the moment we take our first breath until we take our last.

I have rather strong thoughts on TRUE education. Lifelong learning should be one of a person's personal "healthy habits." Getting a bachelor's degree, or a master's, or doctorate does not necessarily mean you are ready for life. I believe that education is something that we DO, not something that we have. Children being taught how to take tests so that they can score better than their peers is a joke in my world. "Let's teach children the tricks so they can do well." That's NOT education, people! Education is pursuing a new understanding of facts and knowledge so that in putting those truths into action, we might become wise in the living of our lives.

I'm so happy that my curiosity makes me a perpetual, lifelong learner. I'm not nosy and curious about other people's business; I'm curious about learning new skills and understanding how things work. Every day I want to do SOMETHING that is new and fresh to me. I get side-tracked by this curiosity a LOT, but it sure does make my life an interesting place to be!

I've heard Chuck Swindoll say that as Christians we have no reason not to be energetic and enthusiastic about everything that we do. If we are in Theos, or in God, which is the definition of enthusiasm, then we have every reason to be full of joy and energy! If we truly are in God then we have every cause for joy and energy that comes from Him! ("For in Him we live and move and have our being." - Acts 17:28 - NIV)   I want to look to Jesus for my new lesson every day. I want to remember yesterday's lessons, but I certainly don't want to just live off of them. They would become stale fast, and I would not really be living! I want to sit at Jesus' feet and learn every new lesson that He has for me – I want to keep it fresh!

One of the reasons we are so big on home education is that we love the concept of the older ones teaching the younger ones, and the younger ones being put in a situation where they can learn from the older ones. For example, when our children were young, instead of having a birthday party with a room full of twenty eight-year-olds, we would host a party and invite the entire families of each eight-year-old and make it a family friendly event. The older ones would help us with the younger ones and the events were always great fun!

One thing about life, that you've probably noticed is that it never stays the same. Life changes constantly, and as the years pass we continually have new lessons to learn and new challenges as we go through different periods of life. We are born, we are young, we attend school, we marry, we have children, our children marry, we become grandparents, our parents become elderly, we age ourselves, and then we prepare to die. It will be the ongoing cycle of life until the Lord returns or calls us home to be with Him. One of the hardest lessons to learn is how to gracefully transition from one part of the cycle to another. When our first child married, this is what I wrote in my diary.

"My baby is getting married tomorrow. It is sweet and hard and good all at the same time. I'm going to have to grow up if I'm going to let my baby go."

Well, according to the law of the land, I had been grown up for more than 25 years, but I didn't feel like a grown-up in that moment. When both of a person's parents pass away, they reconcile themselves to the fact that they are now the older generation. And what's it going to be like, to be a grandmother? I have that to look forward to and so many other lessons. Once I wrote in my diary,

---

"I wish I could start all over again, and do it right this time."

I can't remember what that was about, but I was certainly acknowledging that I had messed up something and recognizing that I could not go back in time. Time keeps rolling and stops for nothing. I want to get as much right as I can with the Lord's help. I fall upon His mercy for the rest. He alone knows how much I have messed up.

Whatever I'm already good at, I want to continue to fine tune my craft and get better at it. Why be content with staying the way I am? To savour life with enthusiasm, I want to keep getting better! There's a thrill that goes along with learning new things, so why ever be just satisfied with the way things are? That just sounds boring to me! And when we mess up, let's laugh at ourselves! We do know how to laugh at ourselves. We are not afraid to look silly. When we mess up, we might as well laugh hard, and learn well, right? The most amazing inventions were often fine-tuned after years of seemingly hopeless mistakes and error. Look at Thomas Edison. His teachers said he was too stupid to learn anything. He was fired from a few jobs because of his unproductivity, and it took him at least 1,000 attempts, before the light bulb was a success.

One of the most significant lessons I have learned, is how far I can push my body to great lengths (at least for me). I have developed an inner resilience throughout my long illness. Before, when I felt bad, I would just have to go to bed. Now, I have learned that if my mind is willing and my spirit is strong, I can do so much more! Great athletes learned this lesson long before I did. Olympic competitors push their bodies through great pain at times to achieve their goals and win the prize, when others would think that the pain was not good for them and stop the activity. There have been many stories of a person on their deathbed, hanging on, until they could say goodbye to a particular loved one or impart specific last words to someone. The will is a powerful tool and when combined with a mighty spirit, can accomplish great things!

Here's another diary excerpt on learning.

"It's just starting to get cool again, here in Georgia. I've been able to turn off the air conditioning, and put socks on my feet. After a busy summer, I'm trying to settle into "my new normal." Dad, Frank Jr and Tara all went to Heaven in a space of three weeks. I'm learning how to parent grown-up kids. I'm learning how

> to teach piano and voice well. I'm learning how
> to live with a chronic illness. Not me, this time,
> you understand, but another family member.
> And how to walk through trials and
> be better for it."

The key here is to note that as long as we are alive, on this earth, there will be suffering, pain, lessons and learning. I am going to ask the Lord today, what He would have me learn from Him? Today is a new day that can only be lived once. I don't want to waste a minute of it.

Below are some questions that I would like you to answer. Please engage and allow yourself to be brave.

Are you an intentional learner? _____

What are you going to be intentional about learning today? e.g. a new skill – cooking, music, an exercise regime, a writing skill, or . . . _____

_____

_____

_____

_____

Are you going through a real-time trial today from which a life lesson can be learned?   If so, what is the trial?_____

_____

_____

_____

Have you any idea what the Lord might be wanting you to learn as you walk through this difficult time?

_____

_____

_____

_____

Chapter, the Thirty-second.

A Passion for Worship.

"One day older, another moment past. Living in eternal life where promises will last. My hope and faith are growing. My eyes are on the goal. Jesus, every breath I take, for You and You alone."
(Walk by Faith - VHG)

We were created to worship. There is a deep longing in the heart of everyone to worship something or someone. According to Webster's dictionary, the definition of worship is "reverence offered to a divine being or supernatural power." It is also defined as "an extravagant respect or admiration for or devotion to an object of esteem". But what exactly do we worship? People in the 21st century worship many things. Money. Power. Appearance. Health. Good looks. The Right to Happiness. Respect. Or _____? You fill in the blank.

God created us with an inner desire to worship Him. The only problem is, some of us have not learned this yet, and are still trying to fill the empty place inside of us with something other than God Himself. It will never work. Only God can fully satisfy our hungry souls. Do you ever just feel lonely, or incomplete, or unsatisfied? That is a need that only God can meet. We come to Him to worship Him in spirit and truth. That means that we intentionally fill our minds with His Word. We also let His Word come out of our mouths, when we sing to one another in Psalms and hymns and spiritual songs. We teach one another the Bible, or listen to the Word being preached by a pastor or an evangelist. The point is – worship is all about experiencing truth, and letting the truth permeate who we are, and therefore what we do.

The Lord values our worship. In fact, He gave Himself to the Levites as an inheritance. The Levites were the tribe of the Israelites who were in charge of leading God's people in worship. God was the focus of their service, their sustenance, and why they got out of bed every morning. God did not give the Levites land, He gave them Himself. This is huge in understanding what worship is. Worship is not about music. It is about focusing on our God and giving Him the praise, attention, obedience, respect, love and devotion that He deserves. I can worship God while I'm emptying the dishwasher, as well as driving through the rain to get groceries or visiting a sick friend. I can worship the Lord while I am singing with other believers in a church building or while I am teaching piano lessons. It is the attitude of my heart towards God and the desire in all that I do to worship Him. Only Him.

I was born to make music. I started saving pennies for a piano at the age of six. But it was much, much later that I began to understand the role of music in real worship. As Ernie & Debby Rettino said with their creation of *Psalty, the Singing Songbook* - "You can sing songs until you're blue in the face, but if it's not from your heart, then it's not praise!" Worship is giving to God what is rightfully His – worship, adoration, and praise. We can do this anywhere. Shadrach, Meshach and Abednego did it in the fiery furnace! We can do it by simply agreeing with God that He's God and we're not, and that He knows what's best for us.

Does music have a place in worship? Absolutely! The Scriptures are full of stories and admonitions to sing and make melody in our hearts to the Lord. Sometimes I will write a new song of worship to the Lord just for my own personal time with Him. No one may ever hear that song, but I offer it to the

Lord with a grateful heart for all He has done for me. Other times songwriters get to know people they don't previously know with the express purpose of learning their stories so they can write their songs. We totally need to be writing new songs for the church of God. God is working among us every day, and teaching us more about Himself, from His Word, and we need to help give God's people a voice and a song to sing back to Him!

Worship is something that you DO, not something that you watch. When I am writing a cello part for a church service, I am worshiping God. When I score vocal parts, I am worshiping God. The performance part is about leading the church of Jesus Christ in worship to God. When I am creating, that in itself is worship for me. I love to organize whole programs that help to focus the Church on certain aspects of God's character. My passion is to pray, asking God to direct my thoughts and my steps, and to put a program or a service together that will point to Christ. I first started doing this more than 30 years ago on the Priority Team and it is still my passion. I love to see how the Lord brings all things together as we pray and seek His face. I cannot tell you how many times every song, every Scripture reading, every testimony, and even the preaching has dovetailed to make a perfect symphony of truth when there has been no discussion, only prayer about the program in question. I'm a believer. God wants us to look to Him for direction, and He will always lead us.

Remember how the Israelites were told to follow the cloud in the sky? (read Numbers 9:17 - NIV – the cloud symbolized God's Presence.) If the cloud moved, they were to follow it. If the cloud did not move, they were to stay camped there until it did. It was as simple as that. The Lord wants to lead His people, if they will listen to Him. Of course we must stay in His Word because He will never tell us anything contrary to His written Word. The Spirit of God will always lead us to the Word of God.

No we're not always encouraged, and so the church of God needs songs about "lifting up their heads" (Psalm 24) to Him as well. I wrote in my diary not too long ago,

---

"Choosing to smile. Choosing to make music.
But so sad deep down. Just tired and want
some joy in the middle of this journey.
Lord I look to You."

I am convinced that real worship comes out of being honest with God. When I play the piano, I ask the Lord to take my hands and put them where they need to go.   And I ask Him to use me.   Somehow.   This is not about me. Yes, I write music, sometimes to remind myself of the Truth. Sometimes I write it to communicate truth to others. Sometimes it is an expression of praise to the God who is everything to me. The Bible talks about singing a new song to the Lord.   (Psalm 96:1 - NIV)   Laura Story, singer-songwriter of *Blessings*, said, "Making new songs is like a window into Heaven." She's right, of course.   A songwriter pens a song of worship when they have had a glimpse of God's beauty or His Truth, perhaps in a way they have never understood before.

I'm thankful for all the modern day "Levites", who are writing the worship of God's people, giving voice, if you like, to the experience of the Church, today. We are creative because we are made in the image of a creative, Creator God. Whether you are preparing a testimony, a music lesson, collage of photographs, or a song, remember that it can be an expression of worship to our amazing God.   He made us in His image, and we, therefore, can also be creative.   Let's honour Him with our talents and with the strength that He gives us to serve Him.

Beethoven once said, that "to play a wrong note is insignificant; to play without passion is inexcusable." Did he know the Lord Jesus Christ personally?   I don't know, but the writer of Colossians also said, that whatever we do, to do it with our whole hearts. (Colossians 3:23 - NIV)   When I make music, I want to be invested in each song 100%.   No holding back. The Lord looks at our hearts and I don't want to be half-hearted about any music that I make. It is for Him, all for Him.

A diary excerpt:

"I sang a song, today - *Redeemed.* I beat myself up for 2 days for doing such a lousy job. Really it was just me losing sight of my freedom in Christ, and what I had been singing about! Anyway, a sister in Christ said the best thing ever to me – she said it was so wonderful. It was like she was singing the words to the song (and not me). Like it was the cry and expression of her heart (and not mine).
Thank you Jesus."

This is what happens when we give our worship and our small, feeble efforts to Him. He uses them for His glory and to lead people to Himself. It is not our work at all. But isn't it amazing that He would choose to work through us, when we surrender ourselves into His care?

Take a moment to consider the following:

What (or Who) is the object of your worship today?

_____

Do you understand that worship is something you do, or are you merely a worship watcher?

_____

What can you do today to bring an offering of worship to the living God? _____

_____

_____

_____

_____

Chapter, the Thirty-Third.

A desire to teach others.

When I acknowledge all of the people who have poured into my life, it makes me want to give back. If I can reach out and teach others, even a portion of what I have been privileged to learn, then I want to take that opportunity and do just that.

If we are going to teach intentionally, we must both take opportunities and make them. How can I set up my daily life intentionally to help and teach others? When I trained to be a preschool teacher, and then worked as one, I would be very intentional when I set up my preschool room every morning. I knew what I wanted to teach that day, and I set up my room accordingly. I did not make the exact same preparations every day and just hope that new learning would happen.

If I wanted to teach about the human body, for example, there would be storybooks about the body, dress-up clothes out, colouring sheets that related to body parts, a body lesson for circle time, and music that related as well. Even my words to direct their activity would relate to their body parts. I would say, "Walk with your feet and take your bodies to line up at the door for snack time," or "Please use your fingers to take a piece of fruit and then use your hands to pass the tray," and on and on it would go. There was a strong focus that day on whatever we, as a staff, wanted to teach. We were intentional.

Everyone needs a schedule – a PLAN. For my own children I kept a current list of random INSIDE activities. The list would look something like this: knit for dolls, sew, paint, read, listen to books being read, mommy tapes, make playdough, baking, make cards, make paper, write letters, play instruments, sing, play pretend, puppet shows and so forth. Our list of random OUTSIDE activities looked something like this: skip, hammer and nail, paint the fence (with water), sand box, tea party picnics, Chinese skipping, going to the park, riding bikes on the pavement, walking to the library etc. Once a month we would sort all of our toys, so that it was like getting new ones every month. I think we ended up with about six boxes of toys in the attic, which meant that most toys were only seen once every six months. It was the best activity ever, AND it kept their rooms tidy!   It was a win-win for everyone!

Every year were children's camps, football camps, Bible conferences, Christmas programs and home hospitality, all which offered excellent opportunities to teach others. Some questions I often ask myself are, "Am I being generous? Could I be giving more?" and "HOW can I be more generous?" Teaching is generosity because it requires that you give of yourself. I am not a gifted teacher, but I realize that teaching is about relationships, and pouring myself into someone else's life.   It is loving, expecting nothing in return. Now that I have music students, I so want to be that role model that so many people have been to me. I want to encourage others to love to learn also. Because of the hundreds of people who have poured into my life, the least I can do, is to do the same for others!

So, we purposefully make opportunities to teach others and **unintentionally we are teaching all the time.** People are seeing us and watching us as we live life alongside of them. When you have children of your own, you realize that everything you say and do will be copied.   Therefore, many people, at this point in their lives, will begin to carefully examine what they believe, how they are spending their time, and what they value the most. They know that it's no longer just "about them," and the responsibility of caring for another human life makes them realize that it's time to "grow up!" Children watch us so closely and learn our bad qualities as well as our good qualities. That's a scary thought, but it's even more frightening when you see one of your less honourable qualities being mirrored in the life of your child for the first time! What we can pray for, and the best scenario, would be that other people will see us enjoying our God and will want to know Him too.

What drives us to teach, especially if we are not teachers? I NEVER thought I would want to teach but yet I have been teaching all my life. For me, it was my purpose in life that was connected to a spiritual gift that God had given me – encouragement and exhortation. I am driven by a passion to encourage others, and so I teach. Life is full of teachable moments. When a child comes to sit on my bed at midnight to talk about their day or when I am tucking another into bed, and they ask me why rain falls downwards or if the moon is made of cheese, it is an opportunity. When we are at the dinner table and someone asks me where peanuts come from, or when I get asked, "Mommy, why was that lady at the grocery store so angry?" These are all teachable moments. It says in Deuteronomy 11:19, to impress the teachings of God on your hearts and your souls, and to teach them to your children when you sit at home, and when you walk along the road, when you lie down, and when you get up. (paraphrase mine) I may have a plan for my day, but some of the best teachable moments I've experienced were not planned. God opens a door of opportunity and it's important that we see it as that, and not just as an interruption.   Consider the following:

What is your one driving passion for life?   Describe in as much detail as possible. _____

_____

_____

_____

If you're saved, what spiritual gifts has the Lord put in you, for the edification of His body, the Church?

_____

_____

_____

_____

Are you willing to use your influence to teach others? _____

Are you being intentional about teaching others?

_____

_____

What opportunities do you have in your life today to see and use teachable moments to help others?

_____

_____

_____

_____

Chapter, the Last.

The Common Thread.

For many years, I had the privilege of being program director and theme and music chooser for our church. After more than 15 years of doing it, I never stopped being amazing at how the Lord would tie together, the scripture reading, the songs, the sermon, and what people needed to hear.

Often the Lord teaches His church a similar lesson, all around the world. The Church of Jesus Christ is taught by the Holy Spirit Himself, if we are listening. And as I've mentioned before, the Spirit of God will always lead us to the Word of God. Songwriters for the church are often writing about similar themes in any given period of time. God has a message for His church, and He puts it on the hearts of many, many people, so that it will get communicated and be heard through song, the spoken and the written word.   He does not want His message to be missed. God is at work, and we must pray, and ask to be shown where He is at work, so that we can be involved too! Let's not miss what God is doing!

Here's a life example of when I did not LISTEN to God. I purchased a CD for a friend - let's call her Mary.   The Lord spoke to my heart and told me to give it to Betty instead. I went ahead and gave it to Mary anyway. Duh! Mary already had it.   So THEN I went and gave it to Betty, but the first joy of obedience was gone.   I missed the greatest blessing. Why am I so hard of listening? I don't know if the CD ministered to Betty or not, but I know that I had learned a valuable lesson. Stay close to Jesus. Listen for His voice.   Stay in His Word daily.   Remain connected to the Vine.

"I am the vine; you are the branches. If you remain in me and I in you, you will bear much fruit; apart from me you can do nothing." (John 15:5 - NIV)

The Lord knows how reticent I often am to follow His leading. I love it when He nudges or even PUSHES me in the right direction! I am not a "charismatic", but I do believe that God is so much greater than any doctrine of God that we could try to squeeze Him into. Let's learn to hear His voice. Who knows what great adventure He has waiting for us, just around the corner!

Education is pursuing a new understanding of facts
and knowledge so that in putting those truths into
action, we might become wise
in the living of our lives.

Closing thoughts.

So what's this all been about anyway? It's about recognizing that I am slow to understand the ways of the Lord, but that I WANT to be teachable. I want to know my God. I want to trust His heart, His ways, and I choose to adjust my thinking to His. I have wasted time, and I don't want to waste any more.

On the 4 March 2015 I wrote in my diary,

> "An adventure is coming.
> Get ready to step into it and to Trust God!"

I had no idea that a book was going to be written. I had no idea that I would be writing more music and getting a grand piano and traveling back to the UK with my husband. I just knew that something new was on the horizon and that I needed to be ready to trust God.

If I had known, 35 years ago, that I would have a family that travels to India, Canada, all over the UK, Haiti, and other places that can't be mentioned, for the sake of the gospel, I would have not been able to take it all in. I have read through years of diaries, asking the Lord what I was to share in this book. I have had many interests, passions, hobbies and studies over the years, but the one constant that I see in every page of every diary is this prayer:

"Lord, please give me a heart to KNOW You,
and to LOVE You."

May this passion continue – I want to end this earthly journey well.

My deepest prayer for you, reader, is that you would seek to know your God and trust His ways. That you would not waste any more time. Do what He is calling you to do. Today. And *Step into the Adventure* that He has for You.

It'll be good, I promise.

Epilogue. A Personal Plea.

Just between me and you, dear friend,

(I can call you friend right? You did read my book, after all.)

If you have never come to the place in your life, in which you realize that you are a sinner, that you need saving, and that Jesus Christ is the only One Who paid the price for our sin, and therefore has the right and the ability to save us from ourselves, and put us on the road to Heaven, let me plead with you.   Be reconciled to God.   Not in a year, or ten years, but TODAY.   Put your trust in Him.   He longs to have a relationship with you.

You cannot even know what the next hour holds for you, but you can know THIS.   That if you have put your trust in Jesus Christ, that you have a home being prepared for you in Heaven.   You will never have to face death of the soul and spirit.   EVER. If you put your trust in Christ, and His atoning sacrifice for your sins, on the cross, when your body dies, you will simply be transported from this world into the Presence of Christ, in all His Glory! It says it all in the Bible. I've read it. I've personally trusted Him, and I can promise you that He never breaks His promise. EVER. He is God and we are not. The wisest decision we could ever make is to respond to Him as He calls our Name, put our trust in Him alone for our Salvation, and believe His Word.

If this is hard for you, and you feel like you just aren't ready to take that step of faith, then I encourage you to pray to Him. Tell Him how you feel, and ask Him to reveal Himself to you. He promises that He will answer those who call on His Name.

You can also get into the Bible for yourself. I suggest you start reading in the Gospel of John. It's a little more than half way through the Book – but trust me, it's a great place to start!

Personally, my absolutely favourite book of the Bible is Hebrews. I like Hebrews because it talks about Jesus being better than all of the old way of doing things, and better than us trying to please God with our good works.

Hebrews 7:25 says, "Therefore He (Jesus) is able to save completely those who come to God through Him". *(NIV)*

So, basically, the first six chapters of Hebrews explain the case of WHY Jesus is able to save us. That's what the "therefore" is there for, to tell us how He has earned the right to save us if we will put our trust in Him! Read it for yourself. It's all there. Let's break this one verse down by asking some simple questions.

Thinking of Hebrews 7:25.

Who? Jesus is able to save. **Who?** All who come to God through faith in Him.

When? When they draw near to God.

What? Jesus is able to save us completely!

Where? Near God.

Why? All need to be saved. He wants everyone to be saved.

Hebrews 7:25 says, "Therefore He (Jesus) is able to save completely those who come to God through Him". (NIV) Yup. It says it all right there.

See how simple Bible reading can be? Ask these five questions when you look at a verse or a passage, and you'll be amazed at what you see that you've never seen before. I like to look at a whole chapter at a time, if not an even larger section. It's important to see the context of who the writer was writing to, as well as the cultural setting and why the writer was writing. And I always like to stop and pray before I read, asking God to open my eyes to His thoughts.

Your life can be secure.

I Thessalonians 2:13, in the new Testament, says it so clearly.

"When you received the word of God which you heard from us, you accepted it not as the word of men, but for what it really is, the word of God, which also performs its work in you who believe". *(NASB)*

It's that simple. When we accept the Bible as God's Word, not men's words and opinions, it will perform its work in us who believe it! I've experienced it. Every time I look into the Word of God, my soul is fed, and I am renewed in spirit. It's not magic, but it's REAL. It's not superstition, but it IS

supernatural.   God is at work in me.   It's amazing.
But please don't miss that first step, and it must be
first.   The first step is the part where I acknowledge
that I am a sinful person, who needs to be saved by
a righteous and holy Saviour.

Ecclesiastes 8:8 declares that **"no human being has
control over the day of his death"**. (ISV) Our days
are limited.   We will probably not know how long
we have on this earth, but it's okay!   If we are ready
for the next life and ready to leave our earthly
bodies, then we have nothing at all to fear. Imagine
that. If death itself can not harm us, what is there to
fear? Put your trust in the Lord Jesus Christ today.
Agree with Him, that you have sinned and that you
need His help. Tell Him that you know Jesus died
on the cross to pay the price for all your sin, and
that you believe that God raised Him (Jesus) from
the dead. Trust in Him and you will be saved.
Right now. This moment.

Here's a poignant quote from an old episode of *The
Twilight Zone.*   "Only if a man lived forever, could
there be any point in living at all."   Yes, when the
writers of the Twilight Zone were exploring so much

that was confusing to the human mind, they came up with this brilliant statement. It's true isn't it? What would be the point of living if we could not hope to live forever? The end is despair, darkness and the grave. When we put our trust in Christ, we have the assurance that our life will never end. In fact, it is only just beginning. Just imagine. Years of learning and growing and experiencing life that never ends.

My husband sometimes reminds me that to say that a body has a soul is actually backwards. Our soul has a body - a temporary body, provided for our soul to inhabit whilst we are on this earth. The physical body will die, but the soul will live on. So we had better make sure, friends, that we are ready when the time comes. I want to make sure that you know how you can know that you have eternal life, and that you will go to Heaven when you die. You really can know.

If you'd like to know more, please contact me. All of my contact details can be found at the back of this book. I would love to speak with you about this most important decision of your life.   This decision affects every other decision!

"These things I have written to you, who believe
in the Name of the Son of God,
In order that you might know
that you have eternal life."
1 John 5:13 (NASB)

Random Life Out-takes.

Vignettes. In case you were wondering.

White Rock's best kept secret.

At the end of Thrift Avenue, a normal little street about 20 houses long, was a hidden garden. You would walk, or ride your bike to the end of the road, and would see what looked like a woodsy area. But as you drew closer, you would see a rickety set of stairs that led below. Go down the stairs and a whole world would open up to you. Trees, flowers, and paths that were mostly undiscovered. In truth, the ravine went all the way from Centennial Park and the Ice Rink, all the way down to the ocean. It was like a little world down there, and it was my Narnia. One year we had so much rain, that it became a mud bath. A person would go down there at their own peril and the deep mud looked like quicksand, out of which the towering trees were moving and swaying as though their very roots were being shaken, and they could fall at any moment. It was a beautiful world, and it was mine. You rarely met anyone else down there. It was private, secretive and silently beautiful. It was where I went to dream.

The Man on the Tracks.

Back in the 1950s, Mom and Dad rented a little house on the west end of Marine Drive. It overlooked the ocean, on the water's side.   The house is still standing there.   Every day the train would pass through White Rock. It came from the United States, and went into Vancouver and beyond. There was a man who would drink too much.   My dad would see him down on the tracks and go down to move him off of the tracks before the train would come. More than once, my dad saved this man. But one day, dad wasn't there to save him. It just goes to show that you can lead a horse to water but you can't make him drink.   Some people will not learn from their mistakes. You can present them with the facts and they will not let that information make them wise.   We can do our part, but unless a person is willing, they will not apply that wisdom to become a better person. This is one of life's history lessons that I had to learn from as I was growing up. When you have an opportunity to learn, take it, because the chance may pass, and it will be too late.

The Hall Family Band.

Dad was a musician to the core of his very being. Music spoke to his soul. He grew up in the Salvation Army playing euphonium alongside of his siblings and cousins and friends. It was a way of life. His own father, at that time the bandmaster, grew up in Bolton, Lancashire in England. They would work in the mines for 12 hours a day, and when they came up out of the mines, they made music. Dad carried on this tradition with his family. He taught each of us an instrument and a repertoire of music, and every Sunday night we would do a concert in a church, somewhere in the lower mainland. Dad played euphonium (and was an artist), my mother played the tenor horn, Wendy & Debbie played cornet, Brian played the Eb bass and Randy played the drums. When I came along, I got to play the triangle. But this was a culture unique to my home. You can imagine just how much music practice went on every day. We learned discipline from this. One time we were traveling on the way to a concert and Brian said, "Oh no, Dad, I left my music at home." Dad said, "Well, Brian, can you play without it?" Imagine how proud Dad was when Brian said confidently, "You know Dad, I think I can!"   And he did.   My own mother learned enough music to play cornet in the Hall family band. She learned enough piano once to accompany my Dad, when he had a euphonium solo to play, and those piano parts were difficult. I know, because I played them later for him, myself! We were taught that we can do anything we want to, if we set our minds to it!

The kitten.

One evening, at about 9 p.m., my little Heather came to tell me that there was a feral kitten outside under my truck and asked if she could give him some food. An hour later he was meowing LOUDLY by the front door.   We opened the door and he ran in. Oh dear. Now he was scared. So he ran into my bathroom. Anne & Heather shut my door and caught him. He was settling down and purring at that point. Then my closet door made that horrible squeaking sound that it often made and the cat went CRAZY. I heard crying and screaming. I ran into the bathroom and Anne's face was bleeding,

Heather had four teeth marks on her hand, and the kitten was balancing itself on the top narrow ledge of Wyatt's shower. Anne crawled up, wrapped him in a towel and lifted him down, bleeding all the while. At this point, Heather was no longer worried that the coyotes would eat the kitten. She now thought it was a stupid kitten. I heard crashing noises in the basement. Wyatt was bringing up the dog kennel as fast as he could. He put the kennel in the garage and the kitten was thrown into the kennel. Then the internet search began on the subject of cat bites, Tetanus and Rabies. I dressed Heather's wound and then crawled into bed with her until she fell asleep. Crying kitten noises were wafting in from the garage . . . 24 hours later, things were looking a bit brighter in the Gwin household. Heather and Wyatt had been to the doctor and she had survived her Tetanus Shot. Our dog, Shelley, insisted on lying down beside the kitten's crate, in the garage, to bring comfort and solace. We later took the kitten to be neutered only to find out that the he was a she. By the way, the story has a good ending. We kept her as our outside cat and called her Liesl.

The magical power of books.

Books are amazing. They take you to places that you could never dream up in your wildest imaginations. Books help you to think about things that are outside of your life experience. I love words. Other people's experience enables them to use words in a different way than I am able to use them, so that is what makes reading OTHER people's work so interesting. When I was a little girl, my parents had an entire shelf filled with encyclopaedias. I was never bored, because I could read the articles in those encyclopaedias for hours on end. My mother subscribed us to a book club – one book would come in the mail every month. What an exciting day that was! At first we received the entire collection of *Dr. Seuss* books. Later on we received all of the *Raggedy Ann and Andy Stories* by Johnny Gruelle. My favourite was called *The Camel with the Wrinkled Knees.* Doesn't that just grab your attention? I spent hours poring over that book. Books can bring hope. The story of *The Little Engine that Could,* is embedded in who I am as a person because Mom read it so often to me. I can do anything that I believe I can do, right? Going to the library to get my first library card in White Rock was a magical day for me. It meant that the whole world in the massive library was opened to me, if I only walked through the revolving door. Sadly, I have proof of my constant visits to that library. Only last month, I found a book called, *Laurie and the Yellow Curtains* on my bookshelf from the 1960s. I'm sorry, White Rock library. I meant to return it, honest. In the 70s I had freedom to ride my bicycle all over my hometown. Often, it was seen parked outside of the *Black Bond Bookstore*. I was inside perusing the shelves at leisure and delighting in the smell and sounds that can only be experienced in a store full of books. When my children were little, we would walk the 1.1 miles down Dawes road, from our home to the Fulham Library. It was a necessary and delightful outing. We had a big square trolley that we pulled behind us. Each of my four children were allowed to take out six books, I believe, as well as endless videos and cassette tapes. Thus the reason for the trolley. To my knowledge I have returned every single one. There was a lovely librarian at the Fulham library. Her name was Marion, but to us she was Maid Marion from Robin

Hood. Although our favourite bookstore in Chelsea has been closed down, let me describe it to you. There was no place like it. Going to *Daisy and Tom's*, on King's Road was an outing. A real experience. There was a 1950s soda counter, for treats, a hair salon in house and an indoor carousel that children could ride on. Toys everywhere. Like the Harrods's toy shop, with luxury and high-street toys, only more charming!   And the bookstore! The bookstore was a book lover's dream. It was two stories high, with stairs and a walkway all around the second level, which of course, meant books from the floor to the ceiling.   My children and I thought we were in heaven. Another favourite book stop was on Fulham Road in London. I used to go to *Peter Harrington's Antiquarian Books* at 100 Fulham Road, where I would celebrate amazing finds, every time I walked through the door. Leather bound 1930s volumes of Dickens and Baroness Orczy and the smell of mouldy books. You have to be a book lover to appreciate that smell, I'm sure. And now? Yes, I read books on my Kindle sometimes, and I listen to books on *Audible*, but there's still not anything quite like holding a well-made book in my hands.

Check out the back page for all of my contact details.

I would love to hear from you!

Footnotes and credits.

As you would expect.

In alphabetical order.

Audible.com

Austen, Jane. *Emma*. Published May 6th 2003 by Penguin
Books (first published December 23rd 1815) ISBN:
0141439580

Austen, Jane. *Pride and Prejudice.* Published October 10th 2000 by Modern Library (first published January 28th 1813)   ISBN: 0679783261

Beethoven, Ludwig Van; 1770-1827 German, composer

Blackaby, Henry T. *Experiencing God: Knowing and Doing the Will of God.* Published 2009 by Lifeway Press (first published June 1976)

Casting Crowns. *Broken Together.* Recording. Publishing: © 2013 Sony/ATV Tree Publishing (BMI) All rights on behalf of Sony/ATV Tree Publishing administered by Sony/ATV. / My Refuge Music (BMI) (adm. at CapitolCMGPublishing.com) / Songs of Universal, Inc. (BMI) / G650 Music (BMI). All rights reserved. Used by permission. Writer(s): Mark Hall, Bernie Herms

Chapman, Steven Curtis. *All About Love.* Written by Steven Curtis Chapman • Copyright © Warner/Chappell Music, Inc, Capitol Christian Music Group. Released on January 28, 2003, by Sparrow Records.

Chariots of Fire. Movie. 1981 British Historical Drama. Directed by Hugh Hudson. Produced by David Puttnam. Written by Colin Welland. Production Company: Allied Stars Ltd., Goldcrest Films, Enigma Productions and The Ladd Company. Distributed by Warner Bros. & 20th Century Fox. Release Date March 1981

Clark, Mindy Starns. 2007. *The House That Cleans Itself.* Harvest House Publishers. ISBN-10: 0736918809 ISBN-13: 978-0736918800

Dickens, Charles. *The Tale of Two Cities.* Published January 30th 2003 by Penguin Classics (first published 1859) ISBN: 0141439602

Dictionary.com. 2016 Dictionary.com, LLC. Go to www.dictionary.com

Elliot, Elisabeth. *Through Gates of Splendor.* Published October 14th 1981 by Tyndale Momentum (first published 1956) ISBN: 0842371516

Ezzo, Gary and Anne Marie. 1997. *Growing Kids God's Way: Reaching the Heart of Your Child with a God-Centered Purpose.* Publisher: Micah 6:8; 4th edition.

Grant, Amy. *El Shaddai.* Recording. 1982. Produced by Brown Bannister. Written by Michael Card, John Thompson. Myrrh Record Label.

Gruelle, Johnny. *Raggedy Ann and Andy and the Camel with the Wrinkled Knees* (1924) by Johnny Gruelle Publisher: Simon & Schuster Books for Young Readers (September 30, 1993) ISBN-10: 0027375854 ISBN-13: 978-0027375855

Guichard, Jean. *Phares Dans la Temps.* La Jument is the
   name of a lighthouse at the Northwestern part of France.
   It became well known in 1989, through a series of
   photographs taken by Jean Guichard.
   From Wikipedia, the free encyclopedia.
   https://en.wikipedia.org/wiki/La_Jument

Gungor, Michael. *Beautiful Things.* Recording.
   Songwriters: Brian Johnson / Christa Black / Jeremy
   Riddle. Copyrights: 2009 worshiptogether.com songs

permission. All rights reserved worldwide.

Holy Bible, **New King James Version**. Published by
HarperCollins, a subsidiary of News Corps. New
Testament published in 1979; Psalms in 1980 and the full
Bible in 1982.

James, Williams. Psychologist and Philosopher. 1842-1910.

Kent, Carol. *When I Lay My Isaac Down.* NavPress; Exp Upd
edition (September 4, 2013) ISBN-10: 161291442X
ISBN-13: 978-1612914428

Kondo, Marie. *The Life-Changing Magic of Tidying Up: The Japanese Art of Decluttering and Organizing.* Cathy Hirano, translator. Published 2014 by Ten Speed Press. (first published in 2011) ISBN: 1607747308

Lewis, C.S. *The Lion, the Witch and the Wardrobe.* Published in 1950 by Geoffrey Bles.

Love Language Test. Dr. Gary Chapman. The Five Love Languages: How to Express Heartfelt Commitment to Your Mate. Published October 13th 1992 by Northfield Publishing (first published January 1st 1990) ISBN: 1881273156

Macaulay, Susan Schaeffer. 1984. For the Children's Sake. Crossways Books. ISBN: 089107290X

Merriam-Webster Dictionary. **Publisher:** Merriam-Webster, Inc.; New edition (January 1, 2016)
ISBN- 10: 087779295X
ISBN-13: 978-0877792956
Online dictionary: www.merriam-webster.com
2016 Merriam-Webster, Incorporated

Montgomery, L.M. *Anne of Green Gables.* Published 1976 by Bantam Books (first published 1908).

Myers-Brigg. The Myers & Briggs Foundation. Take the test here! http://www.myersbriggs.org

Oakley, Paul. *Jesus, Lover of My Soul.* Copyright© 1995 Thankyou Music;   CCLI Number: 1545484

Ortlund, Anne. *Building a Great Marriage.* Published January 1st 1985 by Fleming H. Revell Company;   ISBN-13: 978-0595226665 ISBN-10: 0595226663

Oxford Dictionary of English, online. Current Online version 2015. Oxford University Press.   www.oed.com

Rettino, Ernie & Debby. *Psalty, the Singing Songbook.* www.psalty.com ; 2014 Rettino/Kerner Publishing

Schaeffer, Edith. 1986. *Forever Music: A Tribute to the Gift of Creativity.* SPCK Publishing. ISBN-10: 0281042497 ISBN-13: 978-0281042494

Schaeffer, Edith. 1985. *The Hidden Art of Homemaking.* Tyndale House Publishers. ISBN: 0842313982

Sole mate socks. Website: www.socklady.com

Story, Laura. *Blessings.* Recording released 2011. INO
Records, distributed by Sony Music Entertainment.

Taylor, Hudson. 1832 – 1905. Protestant Christian
    missionary to China and the founder of China Inland
    Mission – now called OMF International.

The Twilight Zone. 1959 TV series. Ran from 1959 – 1964. Rod Serling served as executive producer and head writer, writing or co-writing 92 out of 156 episodes.

Temperament Test.
http://personality-testing.info/tests/O4TS/

War Room. Movie. 2015 Christian Drama film directed by Alex Kendrick and co-written and produced by Stephen Kendrick. Kendrick Brother Productions partnered with Provident Films, Affirm Films and TriStar Pictures to release the film.

Wilder, Laura Ingalls. *Little House on the Prairie.* Originally published in 1935 by Laura Ingalls Wilder. First Harper Trophy Book printing, 1971.

You've Got Mail. Movie. 1998 Warner Bros. Directed by Nora Ephron, starring Tom Hanks and Meg Ryan.

Contact me at betterthanhappy61@aol.com

or check out my author's blog,
www.vickimousesblog.com to hear more of what
God is doing in our lives and ministry.

You can also find me on:

Twitter: @VickiHGwin

Facebook: Vicki Hall Gwin

Instagram: vickimouse

Pinterest: vickimousesews

SnapChat: vickimouse61

Tumblr: vickimousesings.tumblr.com

Our ministry sites:

www.emmanuelandassociates.org

www.emmanuelandassociates.com

No, I'm not a techy nerd. Not at all.